WADSWORTH PHILOSOPHERS SERIES

ON

MAIMONIDES

Charles H. Manekin
University of Maryland

THOMSON

WADSWORTH

Australia • Canada • Mexico • Singapore • Spain • United Kingdom • United States

Printed in Canada
1 2 3 4 5 6 7   08 07 06 05 04

Printer: Transcontinental-Louiseville

ISBN 0-534-58383-0

For more information about our products, contact us at:
Thomson Learning Academic Resource Center
1-800-423-0563

For permission to use material from this text or product, submit a request online at
http://www.thomsonrights.com.
Any additional questions about permissions can be submitted by email to
thomsonrights@thomson.com.

Thomson Wadsworth
10 Davis Drive
Belmont, CA 94002-3098
USA

Asia
Thomson Learning
5 Shenton Way #01-01
UIC Building
Singapore 068808

Australia/New Zealand
Thomson Learning
102 Dodds Street
Southbank, Victoria 3006
Australia

Canada
Nelson
1120 Birchmount Road
Toronto, Ontario M1K 5G4
Canada

Europe/Middle East
/South Africa
Thomson Learning
High Holborn House
50/51 Bedford Row
London WC1R 4LR
United Kingdom

Latin America
Thomson Learning
Seneca, 53
Colonia Polanco
11560 Mexico D.F.
Mexico

Spain/Portugal
Paraninfo
Calle/Magallanes, 25
28015 Madrid, Spain

Contents

Preface

Moses Maimonides (also known by the Hebrew acronym "Rambam;" 1138-1204) presents us with a paradox. He is thought by many to be the greatest Jewish philosopher who ever lived, yet he did not consider himself to be a philosopher. He praises the life of contemplation, yet he lived an active life in Egypt as rabbi, judge, communal leader, and physician. His major work *The Guide of the Perplexed* is widely regarded as a philosophical masterpiece, yet its subject matter is the principles of religion, and its primary aim, the explanation of some difficult terms and parables in the Bible. The *Guide* was written in Judaeo-Arabic for a small audience of Jews educated in philosophy and classical Jewish writings, yet it not only permanently transformed Jewish thought but influenced philosophers from Aquinas and Spinoza to Leibniz and Levinas. And although Maimonides never wrote a treatise or commentary on philosophy, his writings have attracted in recent years the interest of philosophers of language and science, in addition to philosophers of religion.

On Maimonides is an introduction to Maimonides' thought for college students and for interested lay readers, as well as a short companion to *The Guide of the Perplexed*. The *Guide* can make for difficult reading, even for bright students. Although intended to relieve the perplexity of those who confront the conflicting claims of reason and religion, the *Guide* generates perplexity of its own. The idiosyncratic genre of the work, its obscure structure, and its medieval scientific outlook challenge modern readers to find within its pages something of relevance to their lives.

Readers of this book will be better equipped to meet that challenge. They will learn not only that Maimonides tackles many of Life's Big Questions, but also that he offers guidance on how to approach them, and what to do when our chances of success in answering them seem slight. His position as philosophical "outsider" allows him to comment on the limitations of philosophy, as well as its potential. That is one of the reasons why his work still strikes a responsive chord among modern readers. Another is his intellectual honesty: Maimonides likes nothing less than a bad argument in the service of a worthy cause, as we shall see when we consider his criticism of the theologians' arguments on behalf of the creation of the world and the existence of God.

Because the present study appears in the Wadsworth Philosopher Series, I have tried to make it philosophically interesting, which means that I have tried to engage Maimonides on some of the claims I understand him to be making. But as a historian of philosophy I am more interested in "getting Maimonides right." The first chapter introduces Maimonides and his principal works, especially those of philosophical interest. I discuss some material I consider to be of significance in these other writings at some length. The rest of the book treats various themes more or less in the order in which they occur in the *Guide*.

It is my fervent desire that readers will be inspired by something that they find in this book to read the *Guide* itself, which is readily available in English in a good translation by the late Shlomo Pines (see Bibliography). The difficulty of the *Guide* does not lie in Maimonides' style, which is eminently readable, nor with the arguments, which are clearly formulated, but with understanding and reconciling Maimonides' positions, and with seeing the big picture. I hope that this little book is of some help in reducing the difficulty.

I would like to thank Professors Daniel H. Frank, Menachem Kellner, and Kenneth M. Seeskin for their penetrating comments and criticisms of the penultimate draft. Professor Josef Stern's detailed comments improved the book considerably. Thanks are also due to Dan Kolak, the editor of the Wadsworth Philosopher Series, for his encouragement.

Finally, to Mr. Roy Pinchot, with whom I have discussed Maimonides for many pleasant hours, and who read the manuscript with a keen and discerning eye, I dedicate this book.

1
Introduction

Interpreting Maimonides

A short book would do well to steer clear of scholarly controversies, and, on the whole, the present work will. But even the beginning reader of Maimonides should be forewarned about some of the shoals of interpretation. Readers of the scholarly literature on the *Guide* are faced with a welter of conflicting claims and counter claims. Why is there such a lack of scholarly consensus on basic issues? Maimonides himself is partly to blame. He announces to the reader at the outset of the *Guide* (1.Introduction, pp. 15–20)[1] that he will deliberately contradict himself, that his treatise elucidates "concealed things," and that words written in one chapter are sometimes necessary to explain things in later chapters. Does this mean that there is a hidden or esoteric teaching that Maimonides wishes to communicate only to a select few? How far does the reader have to delve into the text in order to grasp his underlying intention?

That depends upon whom you ask. By way of introduction, I will give an overview of the different ways the *Guide* has been read. For our purposes they can be divided into three readings: the radical esotericist, the eclecticist, and the harmonizing.

The radical esotericist reading

Since the thirteenth century some commentators of the *Guide* have understood the literary techniques that Maimonides mentions in his Introduction to the First Part (especially in his "Instruction with

Respect to this Treatise") to be devices aimed at concealing his true opinions. Their commentaries are intended in part to reveal the "secrets" of the *Guide*, which, it is said, Maimonides took great pains to conceal. Not surprisingly the "secrets" they reveal tend to confirm and match the commentators' own predilections.[2] The Jewish Aristotelians read Maimonides as an Aristotelian, the Kabbalists as a Kabbalist, etc. (I have yet to find a medieval commentator who *disagrees* with a "secret" doctrine that he has purported to uncover—unless he happens to be an opponent of Maimonides!) The view that there is an esoteric meaning of the *Guide* that differs from, and in many instances, contradicts the exoteric meaning, provides those commentators with an interpretative *carte blanche* to claim that if Maimonides said A, what he really meant was B. Often, when counter evidence is adduced, it is dismissed as belonging to the "exoteric" level of the book.

Like any philosophical work, especially any work that tries to deal with competing worldviews, the *Guide* has its share of difficulties. The issue is which difficulties constitute real rather than apparent inconsistencies, and what are we to make of them. The radical esotericist reading of the *Guide* generally assumes that Maimonides was too careful a writer and too good a philosopher not to be aware of these inconsistencies, some of which are intended as deliberate ploys to conceal his true views. Some radical esotericists also seem to assume that Maimonides worked out very early in his life a coherent philosophical system, and then invented a system of devices with which to conceal parts of it. This immutable system is embedded in different degrees in various works.

The radical esotericists don't always agree over what Maimonides wishes to conceal. For some it is a strict naturalism that conflicts with traditional religion; for others it is the impossibility of synthesizing philosophy and religion; still others uncover a deeply agnostic view of the possibility of possessing metaphysical knowledge. All of them share the conviction that what Maimonides writes is not always what he genuinely believes, or what he means to convey to the select few.

Critics of radical esotericism concede that Maimonides did not wish to display prominently some of his more religiously unorthodox doctrines, and that he may have used literary techniques to de–emphasize and perhaps even conceal them. Maimonides famously maintains that the Bible teaches beliefs which are necessary for political welfare (3.28, pp. 512–14), and he may have held that all such beliefs are not true. But there is no evidence that he *himself* intentionally misleads the reader on fundamental issues. Hunting for deliberate contradictions in the *Guide* has proven to be as intellectually persuasive as hunting for numerical codes in the Bible; one generally finds what one is looking for. Still, the radical esotericists, both medieval and modern, have been very helpful in drawing attention to passages in the *Guide* which call for further elucidation, and for focusing on the difficulties of the work.[3]

The eclecticist reading

Other scholars attribute the apparent inconsistencies in the *Guide* to what they consider to be Maimonides' philosophical eclecticism. This group often uses the labels of various philosophical schools to characterize Maimonides' strategies and doctrines, which then are said to vary according to the context. Thus, the discussion of divine attributes, which we shall discuss below in chapter 3, is labeled "Neoplatonist" because it is said to emphasize the ineffable, unknowable nature of God which is considered to be a hallmark of Neoplatonism.[4] By contrast, Maimonides' proofs for the existence of God, and some of the characterizations of God, are labeled "Aristotelian." This approach is often favored by historians of philosophy who like to speculate over Maimonides' intellectual sources and antecedents. Many apparent inconsistencies are explained as resulting from this apparent eclecticism.[4]

What is unattractive about the eclecticist reading is that it makes Maimonides into a rather confused philosopher. To move from a Neoplatonist conception of God to an Aristotelian conception in a handful of chapters is not characteristic of a cogent thinker. Perhaps for this reason there are scholars who *combine* these two readings by suggesting that the Maimonides' philosophical eclecticism belongs to the *exoteric* level of the *Guide*. Underlying this eclecticism is a fairly unified worldview that Maimonides wished to conceal. Indeed, the eclecticism may itself be a strategy of concealment.[5]

The harmonizing reading

A third group tends to downplay the apparent inconsistencies and to discern in Maimonides' writings a more unitary worldview on the exoteric level. In fact, this group tends to minimize the importance of the esoteric/exoteric distinction, if not to deny its validity altogether. This is the approach that has been adopted here. Maimonides, like other philosophers, makes statements indicating shifts in nuance, emphasis, and, over a period of time, doctrine. But most of these shifts are relatively minor and are best explained in terms of their literary and historical context. On the whole, Maimonides' worldview is very close to, but not identical with, that of the Muslim Aristotelian philosophers (*falasifa*), especially Alfarabi (d. 950), Avempace (d. 1139), and Averroes (1126–1198). When Maimonides differs from his Muslim antecedents—as he most clearly does, both as philosopher and as Jew—he is well aware of the difference, and feels compelled to justify it. Although he does not view himself as one of the *falasifa*, their influence on him is enormous, and he does not part company with them lightly. His divergences are almost always religiously motivated, although it is admittedly artificial to differentiate between philosophical and religious motivation in Maimonides.

I present Maimonides in these pages as a consistent thinker, unperturbed by intellectual and religious conflicts, whose innermost thoughts and intentions are expressed in his writings for all to see, some with greater clarity than others. Though by no means a literalist in interpreting scripture, Maimonides claims that there are fundamental principles of religion, and that the *Guide* is a work about religious dogmas.

But while Maimonides constructs his major philosophical work around religious dogmas, he is by no means a "dogmatic philosopher" in the way that term is sometimes used by historians of philosophy, that is, he does not believe that objective certainty can be achieved in all matters of importance. As we shall see, he is confident in our ability to demonstrate the existence, unity, and incorporeality of God, but not in our ability to demonstrate the creation of the world, for which he relies on probabilistic arguments and scripture. Certain propositions are demonstrably true, yet others are not; part of his task in the *Guide* is to instruct his readers which modes of proof are available and appropriate for which propositions, and why.

Perhaps because Maimonides takes both scripture and philosophy seriously as sources of truth, his method in the *Guide* is not preachy or didactic with respect to either, except on certain formal occasions, i.e., the proofs for God's existence, unity, and incorporeality. From reading the book one receives the impression of a thinker who has strong views on certain issues, and who uses philosophy and scripture to ground those views in such a way as to render them consistent and, when possible, certain. But, unlike some dogmatists on the one hand, or some skeptics on the other, there are no sweeping claims for or against a complete systematic approach, nor does Maimonides strike one as a systematic philosopher. The *Guide* is neither a philosophical *summa* nor an encoded handbook for decoding scripture, but rather an investigation of one topic after the other, in a certain order and for certain reasons, always in the light of philosophy and of scripture.

The investigatory, tentative, and even empirical aspects of the *Guide* have not been emphasized sufficiently in the present book because of its length. For an appreciation of those aspects one must read the *Guide* itself.

One line of interpretation that I advance in the following pages is noteworthy, if somewhat idiosyncratic: I claim that Maimonides places a greater emphasis on divine will in the *Guide* and in subsequent writings than in his earlier works, and I speculate that his thought underwent a corresponding change during the period immediately preceding the *Guide*'s composition. It is not yet clear to me whether this new emphasis represents a shift in doctrine, or whether Maimonides simply explicates what had previously been left unstated. I suspect that it is a little of both. In any event, this "developmental" approach to Maimonides' thought is pretty new, and, I may add, rather speculative.[6]

Endnotes

[1] References to Maimonides' *Guide of the Perplexed* will be given in the text by listing part, chapter, and then the page number of the Shlomo Pines translation. Other in-text citations list shortened titles of Maimonides' works, subdivisions, if any, and then the page number of the translation that is listed in the Bibliography. Unless otherwise noted, in-text citations are from the *Guide*.

[2] A complete history and analysis of the radical estericist reading of the *Guide* is a scholarly desideratum. For overviews of the history see Ravitzky 1990. Cf. Fox 1990.

[3] For a trenchant critique of radical esotericism, see Seeskin 2000, pp. 177–188.

[4] See, e.g., Guttmann 1988, pp. 152–182.

[5] See, e.g., Pines 1963, pp. xciii–xciv.

[6] Pines 1986, p. 10, was the first (I think) to suggest a significant change in Maimonides' views from the *Mishneh Torah* to the *Guide*, which he interpreted as a move away from a confident medieval Aristotelianism to a "critical" approach that emphasizes the limitations of human knowledge. In my opinion, the critical approach serves to justify philosophically the new emphasis on Divine will.

2
Life and Works

Early Period

Moses Maimonides was born in 1138 (according to one tradition, 1135) in Cordoba, Spain, to a family of distinguished scholars.[1] His father Maimon was a prominent rabbi, judge, and communal leader, who had studied with one of the noted Talmudists of his generation. We know little of Maimonides' early education. Like others who were born into Spanish-Jewish rabbinical families, he studied traditional Jewish texts along with the works of secular learning available in Arabic. With the Almohad conquest of parts of Andalus and the subsequent persecution of non-Muslims (c. 1141–1147), Moses' family began to wander through Southern Spain and Northern Africa, settling for a period in Fez (c. 1159–1165), a center of Almohad influence. To this day it is not clear why, or how, the family managed to live there: according to Muslim reports the family was forced to convert to Islam; others say that 'Abd al-Mu'min, the Almohad ruler, eased the discrimination against non-Muslims in his old age, or focused his attention on Andalus rather than Morocco. In any event, Maimonides' own encounter with religious persecution at a tender age may have influenced his subsequent attitudes towards forced conversion; in an early letter (whose authenticity has recently been questioned)[2] he displays sympathy with the plight of the converts, although he urges Jews faced with forced conversion to emigrate rather than to succumb.

In 1165 Maimonides' family journeyed to the Holy Land, stopping in Acre, Jerusalem, and Hebron. The Crusades had decimated the Jewish communities there, and few centers of scholarship remained. It is not known whether the family had intended to settle in Palestine, but shortly thereafter (c. 1166) the family arrived in Egypt, where Maimonides spent the rest of his life. He soon was occupied with communal affairs and within a short period of time became an important judge and leader of the Jewish community in Fustat (Old Cairo), and, perhaps, the official rabbinical leader of Egyptian Jewry.

Within a few years of his arrival in Egypt, Maimonides completed his first major comprehensive work, the *Commentary on Mishnah* (c. 1158–1168). The Mishnah (c. 200 AD) is the preeminent code of law for rabbinic Judaism, and it serves as the basis for the Palestinian and Babylonian Talmuds. It had rarely been studied in its own right because the Talmuds provided authoritative commentary; hence most scholars, including Maimonides himself, had chosen to comment on selected Talmudic tractates. Maimonides' clear and logical exposition of the Mishnah won him a measure of literary fame. Like most of his writings it was written in Judaeo-Arabic, the *lingua franca* of the Jews living in Islamic countries. Although the bulk of the work consists of short and to-the-point legal exegesis, Maimonides expands the commentary at several points to discuss philosophical and religious issues.

The most important of these expansions is the introduction to his commentary on the Mishnaic tractate *Aboth*, a collection of religious and ethical maxims of the early rabbis. Maimonides' task in this short treatise, known also as the *Eight Chapters*, is to provide the underlying principles of the rabbis' dicta, their psychological, anthropological, and ethical assumptions, as it were. Since these principles are found not only in Jewish sources but also in the books of the philosophers, ancient and recent, as well as the works of other authors, the reader is exhorted to "heed the truth from whomever says it," regardless of the speaker's national or religious identity. In fact, some of the more technical sections of the *Eight Chapters* are based on the writings of Aristotle and the Muslim Aristotelians, notably, Alfarabi, whose writings Maimonides thought highly of.

Maimonides begins the work by analyzing the soul's faculties and its healthy character traits (virtues) and then proceeds to consider the illnesses of the soul (vices) and the way to maintain its health. His treatment is greatly indebted to the Aristotelian psychological/ethical literature, as is his discussion of the relative merits of the naturally virtuous person versus the person who has to struggle to control his impulses. Other topics in the *Eight Chapters* include the subordination of the soul's faculties to the single goal of intellectually apprehending God, the difficulty of achieving this goal, and the lack of astral influence on the soul's dispositions. These topics are treated repeatedly in Maimonides' writings.

Are Theological Beliefs Within Our Control?

One topic, however, found only in the *Eight Chapters*, sheds some light on Maimonides' fundamental view that the religious law (Arabic: *Shari'a*; Hebrew: *Torah*) commands beliefs as well as actions. In considering the five Aristotelian parts or faculties of the soul—the nutritive, the sentient, the imaginative, the appetitive, and the rational—Maimonides considers where to locate religious obedience and disobedience. To the question "Which faculties are pertinent to the commandments of the religious law?" he answers "Those whose activities are subject to our deliberation and choice." Since we can control our sensations and our desires, at least to some extent, religious legislation addresses the sentient and appetitive faculties (*Eight Chapters* 2, p. 64). By contrast, since we have little or no control over digestion, excretion, growth, and procreation, or over the preservation, retention, and combination of images provided by the senses, there are no divine commandments that pertain to the nutritive and imaginative faculties.

But what of the rational faculty? Can religious obedience and disobedience be located in this part of the soul? Well, presumably this question boils down to another one: whether the activities of this faculty are subject to deliberation and choice. Maimonides' statement bears quotation in full:

> Although there is perplexity concerning the rational part, I say that this power too may bring about obedience and disobedience, namely, belief in a false or true opinion. But there is no act in it to which the terms "commanded act" or "prohibited act" would apply (*Eight Chapters* 2, p. 65).[3]

The rational faculty, Maimonides informs us, is a difficult case. On the one hand, religious obedience and disobedience pertain to this faculty because a person's convictions are part of his adherence to a religion. Possessing false theological beliefs, for example, constitutes disobedience to Torah, whereas possessing correct ones constitutes obedience.

But the mental activity of "believing" or "affirming" is not, strictly speaking, an action, at least not of the sort that can be counted as a commanded or prohibited act. Why not? Maimonides himself does not elaborate. Some commentators have filled in the gap by claiming that the act of affirming a proposition *p* is not a *voluntary* act. We are compelled to affirm the beliefs that we hold because of reasons, right or wrong, that lead us to these beliefs. Since Maimonides holds elsewhere that the performance of commandments must be voluntary, this would explain why affirming *p* cannot be designated a commandment. But the problem with this explanation is that Maimonides holds that Jews are commanded to believe that God exists and that He is one and incorporeal. Moreover, if voluntariness is a necessary condition for commandments, then why doesn't Maimonides treat the rational faculty like the nutritive faculty and exempt it *entirely* from religious obedience and disobedience?

Apparently what counts for Maimonides is not so much the activity of deliberation that leads up to the affirmation of a certain belief, or even the mental act of affirmation *qua* act, but rather the mental *state* of the believer who affirms that belief. When one believes that God exists, or that He is One, one is in a mental state that may be characterized as "obedient to the religious law" even though there is no corresponding mental action on which to pin the label "commandment." Elsewhere in the *Commentary on the Mishnah* Maimonides draws up a list of thirteen "foundations of the religious law," beliefs that are incumbent upon every Jew to hold[4]—the first Jewish thinker to present such an authoritative list, and arguably the first Jewish thinker to make adherence to specific dogmas an essential part of Jewish identity.[5] He intimates that whoever possesses these beliefs is ensured a portion in the "world-to-come" (a rabbinic concept understood by Maimonides as the immortality of the rational soul); whoever denies even one of them has no portion.

This raises a well-known question: Can one be *commanded* to believe anything? No, argues the Jewish thinker Hasdai Crescas (d. 1410), because beliefs are not subject to will, and we cannot be commanded about things over which we have no control.[6] (As today's philosophers like to say, "Ought implies can.") Replying on behalf of Maimonides, the fifteenth-century Isaac Abrabanel argues that while beliefs are indeed involuntary, the preparations necessary to obtain this belief (e.g., education, etc.) are up to us. According to Abrabanel, the command to believe that God exists is really the command to take the necessary steps that will ensure that one possesses the belief that God exists.[7]

But does Abrabanel get Maimonides right here? He assumes, with Crescas, that the performance of the commandments must be voluntary for it to have spiritual value, and that the possession of beliefs is involuntary. Maimonides, it appears, agrees with the involuntariness of belief, but disagrees that all commandments must be voluntary. While all commanded *actions* must be voluntary, commanded beliefs need not be. One has performed (or better: fulfilled) the commandment of knowing or believing that God exists, or that He is one, when one possesses the knowledge or belief that God exists, or that He is one—and not before. That one is led to accept this belief by virtue of the force of reason, or on traditional authority, does not detract from its worth as a belief.

Middle Period

In his next major work, the *Code of Law* (*Mishneh Torah*) (completed in 1178 or 1180), Maimonides attempted to codify "all the Laws of the Torah and its regulations, with nothing omitted." The *Code of Law* is unique among Jewish law codes in its comprehensive scope, logical structure, system of classification, and clear Hebrew prose. But more significant for our purpose, it is the only such code that incorporates philosophical, scientific, and ethical material, most notably in the first volume, the *Book of Knowledge* (or, perhaps, the *Book of Mind*).[8] Maimonides held that the system of laws expounded in the Jewish religion rests on broad truths of a philosophical and scientific nature, and, indeed, that there is a relation of reciprocity between law and philosophy.[9] Living in accordance with the mandates of the religious law helps one to achieve knowledge of eternal truths; achieving knowledge of such truths is necessary for human happiness. Hence, as we just saw, the Law (*Shari'a/Torah*) mandates correct beliefs in addition to right actions, as it proscribes false beliefs in addition to wrong actions.

The interplay between law and philosophy is nowhere more evident than in the first section of the *Book of Knowledge*, the "Laws Concerning the Foundations of the Torah." Here are the first few *halakhot* ("laws"):

> 1. The foundation of foundations and pillar of all disciplines is to know that there is a first existent, that He bestows existence upon all [else] that exists, and that all existents—heavens, earth, and everything in-between—exist only by virtue of the reality of His existence. If He were supposed to be nonexistent, nothing else could exist. But if all other existents were supposed nonexistent, He would, alone be existent: He would not cease to exist by virtue

of their nonexistence. For all existing things are dependent upon Him, whereas He, blessed be He, is not dependent upon them—not one of them. His reality, therefore, is unlike any of theirs. This is what the prophet [means when he] says, "And the Lord God is 'true' [*emet*]" (Jeremiah 10:10)—He alone is true reality, and no other is of a reality comparable to His....

2. This existent is God of the universe, Lord of all the earth. It is He who conducts the [outer] Sphere with infinite, endless power, power that is unceasing. For the Sphere rotates perpetually; and it could not rotate without one who turns it: He, blessed be He, is the One who turns it, without hand or body.

3. That one knows this is a positive commandment; for it is said: "I am the Lord your God" (Exod. 20:2). Whoever adheres to the view that there is a god other than this, violates a negative commandment—for it is said, "You shall have no other god besides Me" (Exod. 20:3)—and denies *the* root; for this is the great root upon which all [else] depends (*Foundations of the Torah* 1:1–3, p. 223).

What do these three paragraphs tell us? The first one says that the ultimate foundation of the sciences is to know the following three propositions: a) that there is a First Existent, i.e., God; b) that He makes all other existing things exist, and c) that all other existents depend for their existence upon the First Existent. Note that Maimonides does not adduce proofs for these propositions, nor for his claim that knowing them is fundamental for science. He probably felt that this would be inappropriate for a law code designed to be brief and concise. Instead, he briefly explicates several key notions pertaining to the concept of First Existent, such as its ontological independence from other existents, and the radical distinction between its true reality (or essence) and the reality of others. In terms of philosophical content and terminology, Maimonides follows the Muslim philosophers, especially Alfarabi, who emphasizes these very notions. For Alfarabi as for Maimonides, God is ontologically prior, independent, and the cause of everything else that exists.[10]

The second paragraph shifts the discussion from the realm of metaphysics to that of physics. The Alfarabian *First Existent* is now identified with the traditional Aristotelian *First Mover*. According to the Aristotelians, all physical movement and change is ultimately related to the rotation of the celestial sphere that encompasses the universe. The sphere is in perpetual rotation, and thus requires a perpetual rotator. (Note that this point constitutes a proof for the existence of a rotator, but not necessarily that of God. In the *Guide* Maimonides will use a similar but lengthier argument to establish the existence of God). Later in the chapter Maimonides implies that this "rotator" is not the deity itself, but a subordinate celestial intelligence brought into existence by the deity for that purpose. But this distinction is of no consequence here. His point is to merely flesh out our knowledge of the deity's role to include its responsibility not only for the existence of things but also for the nature of things, the natural processes of alteration, motion, and change.

Maimonides, of course, could assume that his contemporaries would be familiar with the notion of a celestial sphere in perpetual rotation. Because his modern readers are not, we should explain Maimonides' view of the world a bit, at least as it appears in the next three chapters of the *Laws Concerning the Foundations of the Torah*:

Everything that exists, Maimonides tells us, either is composed of celestial matter and form (e.g., celestial spheres and planets); or it is composed of terrestrial matter and form (e.g., minerals, plants, and animals); or it is pure form (e.g., the separate or incorporeal celestial intellects). Surrounding the earth are the nine celestial spheres in which planets and stars are embedded; these spheres are clear so that it appears from the earth that the planets and stars are all in the same sphere, but actually eight of the spheres have subspheres, some of which rotate around the earth, some of which do not. To explain the rotation of the spheres, it is claimed that each of them possesses an intelligent soul, and it moves through its apprehension of God and one of the nine incorporeal intellects.

Through the movement of the spheres the four sublunary elements, earth, air, fire, and water, are constantly combined and separated; their composition readies them to receive the forms that determine them as substances, and thus the cycle of generation and corruption is effected. The giver of the forms is the tenth separate intellect, which is also responsible for actualizing the human intellect; hence its name, the "active (or: agent) intellect." We shall see below that the active intellect plays an important role in Maimonides treatments of prophecy, providence, and immortality.

Philosophical Exegesis of Scripture

Let us return now to our explication of the first three paragraphs of the "Laws Concerning the Foundations of Torah." The third paragraph shifts from the philosophical conception of the deity to the actual scriptural commandment of knowing that He exists, together with its proof text, "I am the Lord your God" (Exod. 20:1). Here, for the first time, Maimonides cites a Biblical verse in the body of the *Code of Law*. But this raises two questions. First, what does that verse have to do with a First Existent that brings into existence all other existing things, and who is identified with the First Mover of the spheres? And second, why is only the first half of the verse quoted, whereas the second half, "who brought you out of the Land of Egypt, out of the house of bondage" is omitted? Can this omission be explained?

Let us have recourse to the *Guide* to remove our perplexity. Our task is to understand how Maimonides relates the philosophical propositions about God to the verse in Exodus that begins "I am the Lord your God," and why only the first half of the verse is cited. What steps of conceptual translation can we take to get us from the philosophical conception of God to the first half of the verse in Exodus and back?

First: the name "Lord." In *Guide* 1.61, Maimonides claims that of all the names of God, only one, the ineffable name composed of the Hebrew letters *Yod*, *He*, *Vav*, and *He*, (translated here as "Lord"), gives a clear indication of His essence, which is utterly different from the essence of anything else. Maimonides offers the suggestion that the name signifies the notion of "necessary of existence," an existence which is completely distinct and independent of all other existing things, and which must exist. Although he does not use the term "necessary of existence" in the *Code of Law*, he does make the point about the ontological dependence of all things on the First Existent.

Next, the phrase, "Your God." In *Guide* 2.6, we learn that the word "Elohim" (translated here as "God") signifies "Judge," and in 3.52 that the term "Judge" when said of God, refers to His being the cause of "the occurrence in the world of relative good things and of relative calamities, necessitated by judgment that is consequent upon wisdom."[12] These occurrences are often occasioned by the cycle of generation and corruption, which, we learn in *Guide* 1.72, is the result of the circular motion of the heavens.

Finally, "I am," which asserts "existence," according to Maimonides. Putting all this together, the Biblical proof text and source of the commandment to know that there is a First Existent, i.e.,

I am the Lord your God,

may be taken by Maimonides as expressing the following idea:

the entity whose existence is unique in its self-sufficiency ("Lord") and who rotates the spheres in a motion necessary for the cycle of generation and corruption in the world ("your God") exists ("I am").

If this is how Maimonides understands the verse, then it explains why he only cites its first half: the second half, "who brought you out of the Land of Egypt, out of the house of slavery," refers to the deity in its historical and particular manifestation as the god of the Jews. Knowledge of this historical fact, as important as it may be for the Jewish people, would not be considered for Maimonides "the foundation of foundations and pillar of all disciplines."

But surely the *meaning* of "I am the Lord your God" is not something like "the First Existent, who brings everything into existence, and is the cause of the movement of the spheres, exists." Maimonides would agree that the verse does not mean anything philosophical on a plain reading, but on a deeper level, it does. That is because he believes the Torah to be the repository of all wisdom; indeed, that encoded within it are the secrets of existence and of all sciences. These secrets were known to Moses who passed on the explanation orally to his successor, and thus for generations, until they were lost and forgotten among the Jews because of their wanderings and vicissitudes, and their secret nature (*Guide* 1.71, p. 177). They were part of the esoteric lore reserved for only the worthy few, termed by the rabbis of the Mishnah, the "Account of the [prophet Ezekiel's] Chariot" and the "Account of the Beginning," which Maimonides identified in the *Commentary on the Mishnah* as divine science and natural science, respectively.[13]

The task of the exegete schooled in the true science of the Law is to reconstruct scripture's philosophical/scientific meaning. Since Maimonides believes that philosophy provides access to many of the truths of existence, the philosopher can discover those truths independently of scripture, and then reveal them *within* scripture. When scripture can be interpreted so as to indicate philosophical and scientific truths, as in the case of "I am the Lord Your God," then one can do so, provided that one exercises caution, as we shall see below. While there is not a great deal of philosophical exegesis in the *Code of Law* (though more than is commonly recognized), it permeates the *Guide*.

Maimonides' philosophical readings of the Bible are difficult for many moderns to swallow. We tend to treat books as historical documents, reflective of their authors' (and readers') intentions and historical contexts. One of the first to read the Bible in this way was the Dutch philosopher Benedict Spinoza, who explicitly took Maimonides to task for reading philosophy into the scriptures and for making the prophets into philosophers.[14] Even those intellectuals who, unlike Spinoza, believed in the divine authorship of the Torah, tended to take it more or less at its face value, especially after the Protestant reformation focused on the plain meaning of scripture, unmediated by an authoritative tradition of any kind.

Seen in the context of his time, however, Maimonides' approach was not unusual. Reading traditional texts as philosophical allegories was the practice of Greeks, Christians, Muslims, and Jews long before Maimonides. And indeed, philosophical interpretation was only one of several ways that medieval Jews approached the text; kabbalistic and astrological interpretations were other ways. The most important Jewish literary precedent for non-literal interpretation was *midrash* (plural: midrashim), the scriptural exegesis practiced by the rabbis of late antiquity, and the early medieval period. Collections of midrashim provided Maimonides more materials for philosophical exegesis, since he held that many of them also contained philosophical lessons.

Although Maimonides does not hesitate to interpret scripture and midrash philosophically, it is wrong to see the hermeneutical process as a one-way enterprise in which Maimonides reads into the text whatever philosophy teaches. Scripture guides the philosopher to find the truth where philosophy and science may be unable to do so. We shall see below in chapter 4 that the testimony of scripture plays a decisive role in Maimonides' acceptance of the temporal creation of the world, and of the existence of miracles.

How and where one draws the line on philosophical interpretation of scripture is a tricky business, and in the centuries following Maimonides, some Jewish philosophers went so far as to interpret the historical passages of scripture allegorically. It is all well and good to say that when a philosophical doctrine is conclusively proven then we must reinterpret scripture, for "truth never conflicts with truth." But who is to determine what is conclusively proven? (Some of this issue will be revisited below in chapter 3).

From the Code of Law *to the* Guide of the Perplexed

The philosophical interpretation of scripture is one of the chief purposes of the *Guide of the Perplexed*, which Maimonides composed sometime between the years 1185 and c. 1190. From the dedicatory epistle that accompanies the *Guide* we learn something of the circumstances of its composition. A young man from Morocco named Joseph b. Judah ibn Shimon had journeyed to Egypt in hopes of studying philosophy with Maimonides. To impress the elder sage he sent letters and compositions of rhymed prose from Alexandria to Fustat, Maimonides' residence. The strategy worked, and Maimonides accepted Joseph as a student. For approximately two to three years (1182–1184 or 1185) they studied astronomy, logic, and apparently some philosophy. During

15

that time the master increasingly began to reveal to his disciple the meaning of biblical verses and the sayings of the Sages. When Joseph departed for Aleppo (shortly before, it appears, Maimonides' appointment as a physician at the court of the Sultan's vizier in Cairo in 1185), Maimonides resolved to compose the *Guide* for his disciple, and for those like him ([Epistle Dedicatory], pp. 3–4).

From the introduction of the *Guide* we learn that the first purpose of the treatise is to explain the meanings of certain difficult terms occurring in the prophetic books, and that its second purpose is to explain obscure, unidentified parables from the same books. Left uninterpreted, the terms and parables are a source of perplexity for the intellectually sophisticated reader who is committed to the truth of scripture. Such a reader faces a dilemma: if she follows her intellect she will have to abandon the literal meaning of scripture, and this may seem to her to be the same as abandoning the principles of her religion. But if she holds fast to the literal meaning of scripture, she will feel that that has brought harm on her religion and will remain in perplexity. In both cases, it is the literalist approach to scripture that is responsible for "heartache and great perplexity." Maimonides' exegetical task, then, is to forestall incorrect interpretations of the problematic terms and parables and to "decode" their hidden (usually philosophical) meaning.

After this announcement of the treatise's aims, we would expect Maimonides to follow with a systematic philosophical Biblical commentary, at least of the difficult terms and parables. Instead, we are given three reasons why such a commentary is not possible. First, the philosophical premises of such a commentary are too numerous to be provided within the confines of one book. Second, it is impossible to give an exhaustive interpretation of certain parables, and, indeed, forbidden by Jewish tradition to transmit anything more than the "chapter headings" of the "Account of the Chariot" and the "Account of the Beginning." And third, no human, with the possible exception of the prophet Moses, is able to comprehend fully the secrets of divine science and natural science.

These three reasons point to the features of the *Guide* that scholars debate incessantly: its unsystematic presentation of philosophical doctrine, its alleged esotericism, and what some have claimed its philosophical skepticism. With respect to the first feature, Maimonides defends his decision to omit even necessary philosophical material because of length (this is a leitmotif in his writings) and because of potential misunderstanding of the "vulgar" (i.e., the non-philosophers). The latter reason also makes him cautious in revealing the secrets of the Torah more than is necessary, in addition to the intrinsic difficulties in understanding and communicating these secrets. He announces that he will scatter the "chapter headings" throughout the *Guide*, so that "the truths be glimpsed and then again be concealed," that he will drop "hints" to the correct doctrine. He admonishes the reader to examine the treatise carefully, and to connect its chapters together because "the diction of this Treatise has not been chosen at haphazard." And finally, he lists seven types of contradictions to be found in any book; the two deliberate types of contradiction, he informs us, have been used in composing the *Guide*.

As I mentioned in the Introduction, some scholars have read Maimonides' warnings and instructions on how to read the treatise as implying that the *Guide* is itself a highly esoteric work, a treatise with "seven seals," as the historian of political philosophy Leo Strauss wrote. But the textual evidence for radical esotericism (which often leads to methodological anarchy) is slim. Maimonides demands his reader read the treatise carefully and constantly in order not to misunderstand it, and he claims that the book can be read with profit on different levels by different audiences. But nowhere does he imply that he has hidden a secret doctrine, for political or other reasons, or that he plans to mislead his reader intentionally. The deliberate contradictions he employs are due to the requirements of pedagogy or the obscurity of the material (pp. 18–20); in the latter case it is not any dangerous or problematic doctrine that is to be concealed from the "vulgar" but rather the contradiction itself.

If there is little evidence that supports reading the *Guide* as containing an esoteric philosophical doctrine, there is scarcely more evidence in reading it as containing an esoteric Biblical commentary, whose philosophical discussions are there "to clarify, support, and prove its exegetical conclusions."[16] Some scholars have taken to heart not only Maimonides' warnings and instructions mentioned in the previous paragraph, but also his claim that a careful reader will be able to interpret the scriptural verses and parables mentioned, but left uninterpreted, in the *Guide* (Introduction, pp. 6, 14) Such a reader will be able to reconstruct the "true intention" (i.e., Maimonides' understanding) of the Bible, which Maimonides has omitted, and, indeed, artfully concealed. And in some instances, it is claimed that this enables the careful reader to fill in doctrinal gaps which Maimonides omitted, intentionally or inadvertently.

There is much to learn from these attempts to reveal Maimonides understanding of scripture, attempts that began almost as soon as the *Guide* was completed.[17] Certainly there is much to criticize in the failure to take Maimonides' scriptural exegesis seriously as a source for his thought. We may or may not agree with Spinoza that Maimonides read philosophy into scripture, but that does not mean that his interpretation of scripture is irrelevant for our interpretation of him. The difficulty is the speculative nature of these attempts. At best, they purport to show how Maimonides *may* have understood a verse, based on what we already know of his doctrine (cf. our explanation in the previous section of how Maimonides may have arrived at his scriptural proof text for the commandment to believe that God exists, "I am the Lord your God.") The problem begins with the assumption that Maimonides' exegetical method can be absorbed by the reader and then used in places where Maimonides himself was silent. This may be true for somebody who is interested in the philosophical exegesis of scripture in order to relieve her own perplexity. But it will not do for trying to figure out what Maimonides himself means, or whether he reads a certain verse as expressing a certain idea.

This is one reason why the present book does not pay much attention to the *Guide* as a work of scriptural exegesis. The other reason is that the relation between philosophy and exegesis in the *Guide*, and, more precisely, how Maimonides viewed his task as scriptural exegete, is difficult. In the chapters that follow we shall focus on explicating the philosophical doctrines that are taught explicitly by Maimonides, doctrines which in many instances he felt to be taught by scripture. If nothing else, this is where readers should *start* their study of Maimonides.

Late Period

Shortly after the publication of the *Guide*, Maimonides composed the *Essay on Resurrection* (1191), wherein he attempts to lay to rest the reports that he denied the physical resurrection of the dead in favor of the spiritual immortality of the intellectual soul.[18] Those reports had reached him already in the early 1180s, but the matter came to a head when his views were criticized by the Gaon (religious leader of Babylonian Jewry) Samuel ben Eli, and publicly defended by his student, Joseph.[19] In this treatise Maimonides claims that the future physical resurrection of the dead is a miracle that must be believed on the basis of scriptural and rabbinic tradition. Miracles are possible because God has the power to alter nature if He so wills; as we shall see, this accords with the view that God created the world after absolute nonexistence. Nevertheless, the ultimate reward for humans lies in the immortality of their souls rather than in their soul's miraculous reunification with their resurrected bodies. In fact, the resurrection of the dead, like all miracles, involves only a temporary breach of nature; after a period, the bodies will die and decompose once again.

Between 1190 and 1204 Maimonides composed ten medical treatises in Arabic, which later contributed to his fame as a physician throughout the medieval world; some were translated several times into Hebrew and Latin. Of particular interest to the student of the *Guide* is the twenty-fifth and last treatise of Maimonides' *Medical Aphorisms*. Although the work is largely based on the medical writings of Galen (Second Century A.D.), this treatise contains a sharp diatribe against the Greek physician's explanation of divine providence and design. Galen, in his work *De usu partium*, had interpreted the philosophers to hold that God chooses the best design for creation within the limits imposed by nature and matter. By contrast, the Bible is said to teach that God chooses to create whatever he likes, unconstrained by nature. Galen, according to Maimonides, misunderstood both the philosophical and the scriptural views. For the former it is impossible to speak of God choosing anything: the world proceeds necessarily and not voluntarily from God. For the latter, while God can indeed will something contrary to nature (and He does, in the case of miracles), all of his actions are in accordance with wisdom and purpose. Maimonides' point is consistent with his remarks in the *Guide* and the *Essay on Resurrection* and are reflective of the shift to a greater emphasis on divine volition after he had completed the *Code of Law*.

Throughout the adult portion of his life Maimonides was engaged in correspondence with scholars and communities around the Jewish world, and some of this correspondence became famous in its own right, such as the *Epistle to Yemen* (1172), a letter encouraging the Yemenite Jewish community to stand fast against various spiritual threats, including a messianic pretender. These letters offer insight into Maimonides the man, his irritations, frustrations, and pleasures. Perhaps the most famous of his personal accounts is contained in a letter to the first Hebrew translator of the *Guide*, the Provencal Jewish scholar and translator, Samuel ibn Tibbon. Ibn Tibbon had announced his intention of making the long journey to Egypt in order to study with the master. Maimonides dissuades him by giving a detailed description of his very busy work week.

Less well-known is a letter of the same period from an unknown admirer of Maimonides, who claims to have studied parts of the *Guide* but needs further instruction: Would the Master be a guide for his perplexity? He declares his willingness to come to Fustat at night, whenever Maimonides has some leisure time, or if that is impossible, perhaps the great sage can recommend somebody else as a teacher. Finally, he asks Maimonides for advice on what foods to eat that will aid in understanding theoretical matters.

Maimonides' response is as follows:

I have become apprised of the contents of His Honor's letter. God (may He be exalted) should fulfill his wishes and add to his understanding. No doubt he has seen and heard of my responsibilities to the gentiles, and how I am "shattered between daybreak and evening" (Job 4:20). I only return [to Fustat] at night, sick and groaning. Too exhausted to sit, I am only able to lie flat on my back....Were His Honor to come to the House of Study on any Sabbath, it would be impossible for him not receive some of what he hopes to receive from me. Perhaps God will give us an hour of leisure for us to study together and to learn. May God add to his welfare.

Almost as an afterthought, Maimonides replies to the request for "brain food":

Your food should include, when you cannot prepare something cooked, almonds and pitted raisins. And it is not bad occasionally to add the honey of pitted figs, fresh, good, and diluted. May God add to your welfare.[20]

The original letter, with Maimonides' autograph response, has been preserved in the Cairo Genizah, the famous repository of the documents of the Jews of Cairo. When Maimonides wrote it, he was the most famous Jewish thinker of his time. Since his death in 1204, he has arguably become the most famous Jewish thinker of all time.

Endnotes

[1] The biographical details of this chapter are based on Kraemer 2001 and Twersky 1972.

[2] See Davidson 2001, pp. 125–133.

[3] I have altered the translation based on the edition of I. Sheilat 1992, p. 231, n. 4.

[4] 1. The existence of God. 2. His Unity. 3. His incorporeality. 4. His eternity. 5. Worship of God. 6. Prophecy. 7. Mosaic Prophecy. 8. Divinity of Torah. 9. Non-Abrogation of Torah. 10. God's Knowledge of Human Actions. 11. Divine Reward and Punishment. 12. Messiah. 13. Resurrection.

[5] See Kellner 1986, pp. 10–65.

[6] Ibid., pp. 127–129.

[7] Abravanel 1982, pp. 108–110.

[8] Septimus 2001, argues that the Hebrew term "madda'" as used by Maimonides also has the sense of "mind."

[9] Twersky 1980, pp. 359–65.

[10] For suggested relations between Alfarabi's thought and the "Laws Concerning the Foundation of the Torah," see Kraemer 1979.

[11] Reference to change in Guide and Langermann, True Perplexity

[12] Trans. Pines, p. 632. On this passage, see below, p. 89.

[13] *Commentary on Mishnah: Hagigah* 2:1.

[14] *Tractatus Theologico-Politicus*, ch. 7.

[15] See Talmage 1986.

[16] Klein-Braslavy 1986, p. 68.

[17] For a recent attempt published in English see Diamond 2002; cf. the two Hebrew works by Klein-Braslavy in the Bibliography.

[18] See the English translation by A. Halkin in Halkin and Hartman 1985.

[19] The suggestion that the *Essay on Resurrection* was a medieval forgery has been laid to rest with the publication of Joseph ibn Shimon's defence of his teacher Maimonides. See Stroumsa 1999, p. XIII.

[20] This translation is based on the editions of the letter published by D. Baneth 1942, pp. 50–56, and I. Shailat 1995, 2:560–563.

3

Describing and Conceiving God

The first sixty-nine chapters of the *Guide* have one overarching purpose: to provide the reader with an accurate concept of God, one that picks out the entity named "God" and nothing else.[1] According to Maimonides, our mental concepts often represent things that exist outside of the mind. If our concept of God is not accurate, then it fails to refer to God, indeed, it picks out something that is *not* God. And this is tantamount to idolatry, a cardinal sin in his eyes. We may *say* that we believe in God, and we may *intend* to worship God, but if our concept of God is erroneous, then we don't have any beliefs about God at all (1.60, pp. 145–6); something else is the object of our belief and worship.

This concern of Maimonides is in many respects unique to him. Other philosophers generally start with a definition of God that they find uncontroversial and move on to proving God's existence. Maimonides, by contrast, gets around to proving God's existence only in part 2 of the *Guide*, and then he devotes relatively little space to the issue. He spends much more time refining the reader's concept of God, and to a large extent the proofs for the existence of God are ancillary to this project. His central task is to help his readers form an accurate concept of God, a concept that refers to the entity named by the term "God."

To help his readers form an accurate concept of God, Maimonides starts with the concept that the reader already possesses and subjects it to critical examination. If he had been Aristotle, then he might have begun by canvassing what other thinkers have said about God, examining each of their opinions, and then coming up with his own position (He does this with some of the other topics in the *Guide*.) Instead, he begins with the Bible, since the truth of scriptures is axiomatic for him, and perhaps because he assumes that what people think they know about God is drawn mostly from Biblical descriptions of the deity (cf. 1.53, pp. 119–120). But since he believes ultimately that scripture must be interpreted in the light of reason, he does not accept the Biblical descriptions of God as true in their *literal* sense. Rather he employs widely held assumptions about God within the Islamic and Jewish philosophical tradition—that He exists, is one, incorporeal, all-knowing, all-powerful, etc.—and uses these assumptions to interpret the Biblical descriptions of God. For example, when scripture portrays God as a person who possesses bodily characteristics, or performing bodily activities like sitting, standing, walking, etc., these terms *must* be interpreted metaphorically. They *cannot* be taken literally because they would then contradict the widely held, and, indeed, rationally demonstrable view that God is incorporeal. The Bible certainly provides guidance for a correct concept of God, but only after it has been interpreted philosophically.

Maimonides' first task, then, is to neutralize the literal meaning of the Biblical descriptions of God by translating them into descriptions that are philosophically "kosher." By the end of the first forty-nine chapters of the *Guide*, the reader will have learnt to replace the literal Biblical concept of an anthropomorphic God with something completely incorporeal. For example, when the Bible describes God as "standing" it really wishes to teach that God is permanent and enduring; "sitting," that God is stable and undergoes no change. In most cases Maimonides justifies his interpretation of the Biblical terms through appealing to other instances of those terms in the Bible where their meaning is metaphorical. This certainly makes his translation-project a bit more convincing, but it seems that the aforementioned widely held assumptions are more important to him. The upshot of his discussion is that Biblical anthropomorphic descriptions, when understood metaphorically, point the reader towards a true concept of God.

Few readers of the Bible nowadays, even fundamentalists, are shocked by the proposition that God does not have a body (although it should not be taken for granted that such was the case in Maimonides' day). Sunday school teachers routinely teach their pupils that God is not an old man with a white beard. But there are other personal descriptions of God, which, according to Maimonides, must not be taken literally. For example, God is often described in the Bible as possessing emotions such as joy, anger, sorrow, etc., as well as desires. Such emotions and desires imply that He is affected by things outside Him, that He is moved by them. But God cannot be moved by anything, for that would imply passion and change, and God does not receive "impressions and affections," (1.52, p. 116), nor does He change (1.54, p. 125, cf. 2.18, p. 301). So any Biblical descriptions that imply divine passibility or mutability must be interpreted in accordance with the widely held philosophical assumptions that He is neither of these.

If God does not possess emotions, then why does the Bible ascribe them to Him? For the same reason that the Bible sometimes ascribes to God physical properties even though He is incorporeal—in order to make God more comprehensible, especially to the multitude of worshippers, and to point discerning readers to a philosophical truth about God. Emotions are states that motivate actions, and since the Bible attributes actions to God, it attributes also the antecedent states.

To see how Maimonides attempts to purify the Biblical manner of speaking about God, let us look at the following sentence, which is in tune with Biblical theology:

(B) God destroyed the wicked city because of His anger.

Maimonides says that the Bible attributes anger to God when wicked cities are destroyed because *we* destroy things out of anger. (1.54, pp. 125–28). The Bible projects our motivating emotions on to God. But God's actions, says Maimonides, are not motivated by emotions, but by wisdom. Like a just judge delivering a verdict, He is not affected by passion, but renders to each according to his due. So ascribing emotions to God is simply a Biblical manner of speaking. Philosophy purifies our concept of Him by showing us that He is impassible, i.e., not affected by external things. So let us rephrase (B) as

(B') God destroyed the wicked city because its inhabitants deserved it .

But this last point raises a question: Even if we grant (B') doesn't it still imply that God's action is a *reaction* to the city's wickedness? In that case isn't He still affected by something outside Him? Also, if He acts at one time and not at another, doesn't He change? Maimonides would reply that once again we are falling into the trap of conceiving divine agency in terms of our own personal agency. Our acts begin and end depending upon external causes and impediments. God's activity is unitary, constant, and unchanging; it only appears to be multiple because it produces different effects on different objects. Like fire, which whitens, blackens, burns, melts, etc., depending upon the material with which it comes into contact, God's causal activity rewards, punishes, builds, destroys, depending upon the circumstances (1.53, pp. 120–21; cf. 2.18, pp. 299–301). So maybe we should rewrite (B') as

(B") God's eternal activity is such that, under certain circumstances, it brings about the destruction of the wicked city.

But we have still not finished our task of philosophical translation of the Biblical statement. There remains the question of the nature of divine activity, and, in particular, its relation to natural causality. Although this point will be taken up in more detail in chapter 5, we ought to mention it in conjunction with our goal of understanding Biblical descriptions of God's actions. When the Bible says that God destroys a city, does this mean that God somehow intervenes within the natural order and causes the city to be destroyed? Or are God's actions carried out within the natural order? Some scholars think that Maimonides *equates* divine actions with the natural order. One of his statements that appears to support this interpretation begins "If you consider the divine actions—I mean to say the natural actions—" etc. (3.32, p. 524). If this interpretation is correct, then God's actions in the world described in the Bible are best equated with natural causes. And so (B") becomes

(B‴) God's eternal activity is such that, when the inhabitants of a city are wicked, the city will be destroyed through natural causes,

natural causes also being equated with God's actions as decreed by God's pre-eternal, unchanging will (1.10, p. 36).[2] So divine emotions are interpreted in terms of the actions they are said to motivate, and Maimonides implies that these actions occur according to an incorruptible and immutable order (3.21, p. 485).

We shall see in chapter 5 that Maimonides modifies this naturalistic picture to allow for miracles, and for divine reward and punishment that do not proceed according to God's pre-eternal will. But for the moment, let us stay with the naturalistic Maimonides. The move beyond naturalism that Maimonides makes does not appear to affect how he understands most Biblical references to divine actions.

The Problem of Attributes

So far we have seen that Biblical descriptions of God must be interpreted in light of widely held or demonstrable philosophical beliefs, e.g., that God is immutable, impassible, incorporeal, etc. But Maimonides goes much farther in his quest for constructing a mental concept that picks out the entity we name "God." He claims that even after the Biblical descriptions are interpreted philosophically, they are false if taken literally as *descriptions*. For the very notion of describing God carries difficulties with it, and so Maimonides finds it necessary to provide a philosophical account of what we *should* understand when we attempt to describe God.

This brings us to Maimonides' treatment of the problem of divine attributes, one of the most difficult areas of his thought, and the subject of considerable scholarly controversy. Maimonides himself cautions teaching the problem to those untrained in philosophy. In eleven tightly-argued chapters (1.50–60, pp. 111–147) he first shows how philosophically interpreted descriptions of God should and should not be understood, and then he provides his readers with a method for drawing nearer to the cognition of apprehension of God, i.e., for fine-tuning their concept of God. The section is difficult for several reasons, but one is worth mentioning here because it seems to have eluded many scholars.

That difficulty is Maimonides' use of a single Arabic word (*"sifa"*) for what I have translated as "description" and "attribute," and what I shall translate below as "property" (in its contemporary philosophical sense). Now in philosophical parlance descriptions are usually understood as linguistic items, properties as metaphysical items, and attributes as sometimes the one and sometimes the other. Since Maimonides uses only one term, it is not clear on what level(s) his discussion proceeds: the linguistic, the psychological, or the epistemological. Hence some interpreters focus their remarks on the issue of religious language ("How do we describe God?"); others on the psychology of belief ("How to we come to a correct mental representation about God?"); and still others on the knowability of God ("What can we know about God?")

Part of the ambiguity stems from the intellectual antecedents of Maimonides' discussion, namely, the treatment of divine attributes in the theology of the Kalam. The Kalam thinkers composed books in which they debated over how the various Qur'anic descriptions of God should be classified and understood, whether they refer to actually distinct properties somehow related to the divine essence, or to a single notion identified with the divine essence. In arguing over the real or merely descriptive signification of divine attributes, the theologians used the term *sifa* to cover both properties and descriptions.

Initially, like a Kalam theologian, Maimonides uses the dogma of the *oneness* of God to guide and motivate his discussion. For the first several chapters his question is as follows: how are we to understand the divine attributes mentioned in classical sources, given divine unity? He points to the inadequacy of the Kalamic formulations, which follows, in his opinion, from the theologians' insufficient grasp of philosophy. The thrust of the discussion is critical and destructive; we are made to see the difficulties of our ascribing positive attributes about God, especially with respect to divine oneness. Later, the treatment of attributes enters a constructive phase, when he offers positive advice on how to form the most accurate concept of God we can. We will take up both phases in turn.

The Destructive Phase: The Problem of Positive Essential Attributes

When Maimonides affirms that God is *one* he does not just mean that God is the *sole* deity, but also that He is a *simple* unity, that is, he has no parts or aspects. This implies for him we cannot ascribe to God multiple attributes the way we do to other things. For example, if Jake describes Samantha as "lively," "clever," and "forceful," we may infer that Samantha's personality is complex and multifaceted. But if we describe an absolutely simple God as "living," "knowing," and "powerful," how can we avoid the same implication?

One possible way out is to claim that such attributes do not refer to *different* properties of God, but to one *single* property, which can be variously described. We saw above that God's activity is unitary and unchanging, although the Bible describes it as many. Can we say something similar about a unitary divine property, that it only appears as different attributes to us? This was the answer of some of the Kalam thinkers, including the Jewish thinker Rabbi Saadia Gaon.[3] But Maimonides demurs (1.50, p. 111; 1.51, pp. 112–14; 1.56, p. 131). Even if we claim that all our descriptions of God refer to a single property, the fact that the entity singled out is a *property* poses a problem. For a property is always a property *of* something, and for an Aristotelian like Maimonides, that "something" is an underlying subject which differs fundamentally from the property. And even if the property always belongs to the subject there is a *real distinction* between the two. But God's oneness, interpreted now as simplicity, does not allow Him to composed of a substance and a property. Hence we cannot interpret these descriptions as referring to a single property.[4]

Another possible way out is to claim that such attributes do not indicate a property or properties possessed by God but simply stipulate what the word "God" refers to, e.g., an entity to which the descriptions "living," "knowing," and "powerful" apply. Would this solve the problem? That depends on what sort of stipulation we are after. If all we wish to do is to give a lexical definition, say, of the three-letter English word "God" (i.e., "Let the word 'God' mean") then this is harmless. But who is to say that this definition describes accurately the entity

27

named by the term "God"? On the other hand, if we want an accurate, and not merely an arbitrarily stipulated definition of God, then this, Maimonides claims, is impossible. For, according to Aristotle, real definitions explain why things are the way they are and why they behave the way they do. By defining humans as *rational animals*, for example, we say that humans are humans by virtue of being rational animals; their essence is *rational animality*. But God can only be explained with reference to Himself and not with reference to anything else. God is not God by virtue of His being powerful or wise or knowing; rather He is those things by virtue of His being God. To say simply that God is what He is by virtue of being God—while true—does not get us very far! (Cf. 1.51, p. 113).

Nor do the attributes that describe God's actions, which we briefly examined above, provide us with any explanatory insight into God's essence. True, they do not impugn divine oneness, and this makes them attractive to Maimonides (1.52, pp. 118–119). Since one nature can have multiple effects (recall the example of fire that whitens, blackens, burns, etc). there is no problem about predicating such attributes of God. But by the same token they are not of much use in providing us with a concept of God because they teach us nothing about His *nature*.

Now this may seem odd to you. After all, if we take the position that God's *actions* are just and good, then can we not infer something about the author of these actions, that His *nature* is just and good, or (respecting simplicity) something that can be described as "just" and "good"? Maimonides would respond that we could make the inference, but we haven't really learned anything new about the divine nature, just as we haven't learned anything new about fire's nature to burn when we observe that fire burns. What we want to know is the explanation *why* fire burns; we want to understand what it is about fire that, given the right conditions, it *must* burn. While we may be able to do this in the case of fire, we cannot explain God in that way.

Of course, if we could experience, or be acquainted with, God *directly* then we might be able to say something like: "'God' names the entity that I experience(d)." But Maimonides does not allow for direct experience of God, except, perhaps, in the case of the prophet Moses.[5] And anyway, there is the epistemological problem (unmentioned by Maimonides) that if we don't have a prior concept of God, then how can we know that what we are experiencing *is* God?

As for forming a concept of God in the way empirical concepts are generally formed, according to Aristotle, namely, by abstracting them from sensory images retained in the imagination, and then creating higher-order concepts through the abstracting from the lower-order ones, that obviously won't work here. For what sensory images can we have of God?

So Maimonides' first step is to lead us to a dead-end in our project of forming an accurate concept of God. How can we form a concept of what we don't perceive and what we don't understand? What are we to do if we wish to ensure that the term "God" used in the traditional sources, including the prayer book, really refers to God? And how are we to interpret all the Biblical descriptions about God?

The Constructive Phase: The Process of Negation

We cannot acquire a concept of God through defining God, or through directly experiencing Him. So what is left? The first step is to look at the class of descriptions that according to the theologians of the Kalam appear to refer directly to God's essence, attributes such as "living," "powerful," "knowing," and "willing." Let us assume what we learned above, that they do not refer to different aspects of God, or even to one property, but refer directly to God's essence. Can we use these to construct a concept that will refer to God?

Maimonides says no and yes: no, if we take these attributes to mean something similar to what they mean when we predicate them of other creatures besides God; yes, if they do not. For God's oneness implies not merely unity or simplicity but *uniqueness*. There is no relation between God and his creatures; hence He shares nothing in common with them; he is *sui generis*. If that is the case, continues Maimonides, then

> the terms "knowledge," "power," "will," and "life," as applied to Him, may He be exalted, and to all those possessing knowledge, power, will, and life, are purely equivocal, so that their meaning when they are predicated of Him is in no way like their meaning in other applications (1.56, p. 131).

It is not sufficient to say, for example, that God is infinitely wiser than we are. For that still implies that God and we share *something* in common called "wisdom" (although He has a lot more of it than we have!) So when we describe God as "wise," we have to add something like the qualifying phrase, "by 'wise' we mean something entirely different from what we mean when we use 'wise' with reference to us." Or to put it his way, "wise" is a *purely equivocal term* when said of God and of humans: God's wisdom and our wisdom have nothing in common besides the name "wisdom."

Before we see how Maimonides explains the signification of terms like "wise" and "powerful" when referring to God, let us think a

29

moment about the thesis that there is no relation between God and His humans. *No* relation? But the Bible posits a multitude of relations between God and humans: creator, lawgiver, covenant-maker, father, master, and husband. As for the philosophers, Aristotle views God as the *cause* of the world's motion, and so at the very least a *causal* relation exists between the two. Now Maimonides agrees here with Aristotle (1.69, pp. 166–171) although he also holds that God creates the world. How can he then claim that there is no relation between God and anything else?

Once again there is no scholarly consensus on this issue. But it is important to see that the "no-relation" thesis is itself ambiguous. Some scholars push it very hard, saying that Maimonides intends to say that there is no relation of any kind whatever between God and His creatures because God is Wholly Other, hence entirely unknowable and beyond all comprehension. The problem with this interpretation is that Maimonides seems to say a great deal about God's relation with the world, and much of his thought assumes that God is knowable; indeed, he holds that Jews are commanded to know things about God. When faced with these points, the aforementioned scholars must maintain either that Maimonides contradicts himself, intentionally or unintentionally, or that he is speaking "through a certain looseness of expression " (cf. 1.57, p. 133) when he writes about such relations.[6]

Other scholars, including the present one, take a different approach. Given that Maimonides makes all sorts of claims about the relation of God and the world, many of which he considers to be provable, and given that he considers the knowledge of God not only possible but religiously mandated, the "no-relation" thesis should be given a weaker interpretation. And in fact, the Arabic term *nisbah*, which Pines translates as "relation," may better be translated in our context as "proportion" or "ratio." When Maimonides says that there is no relation between God and his creatures, he means that there is no proportion, ratio, or external standard by which one can compare the two. They cannot be compared with respect to a common feature or property, unlike, say, a man and a horse, who are both animals, or a stone and a horse, which are both material objects. God's existence is not comparable with the existence of other things because God's existence is identical with His essence, and not a property added to it. Like his predecessor Avicenna (d. 1037), Maimonides holds that God is necessarily existent and everything else only possibly so. This does not mean that God and other creatures share an essential property, "existence," but differ in whether that existence is necessary or potential. With respect to God, existence is not a property. Rather we understand about God

30

that His existence has nothing potential about it, which allows us to conclude that He exists in a way that bears no measure or proportion to others' existence. Nevertheless, we can still talk about His "existence" as long as we are careful to note in what way it differs from the existence of others.

Let us look at some more of Maimonides' examples of interpreting attributes that putatively refer to the divine essence. The Bible describes God as "one." Now, for the Aristotelians the term "one" often indicates one of the two subdivisions of the category of quantity; the other is indicated by "many." Since God is not a quantity, it is false to say of God that He is quantitatively one; to do so would involve what philosophers sometimes call a category mistake (1.57, p. 132). On the other hand, the Bible says, and philosophy proves, that God is unique, i.e., unlike anything else, and there is a sense of "one" that indicates uniqueness. So when we call God "one" what we mean to say is that He is unique, i.e., unlike anything else. This uniqueness is not a property that is added to His essence (hence, it is not an attribute), nor does it really *explain* that essence to us. But it does describe God in the sense that it *distinguishes* Him from others.

Another example: the Kalam theologians describe God as "eternal." Now "eternal" often indicates temporal priority. But, according to the Aristotelians, time is a property of bodies in motion, and since God is not a body, it is false to say of Him that He is prior *in time* to anything else. When we call God "eternal" we mean to indicate that God does not come into existence at a point in time (1.57, p. 133)

In all these cases Maimonides claims that there is something that exists that is not x (e.g., not corporeal, not finite, etc.); to describe this entity, we may call it "not x," or "y," where y is the negation of x. But whether the form of the description is affirmative or positive, the signification is negative: we are not told what the entity is like, only what it is unlike. By demonstrating what this entity cannot be (the so-called *via negativa*) we are able to construct a concept that: a) picks out, by a process of exclusion, the entity that we refer to as "God"[7], and b) does not explain to us anything about this entity's essence, i.e., why it is what it is. Thus we can prove about this entity that its existence is necessary, *without knowing what it is about the entity that renders its existence necessary.* We can prove that it is not corporeal, *without knowing what it is about this entity that renders its existence not corporeal.* To use Maimonides' formulation, we can learn things about God's *thatness*, his existence, but not about his *whatness*, his essence, which explains why He is the way He is (1.58, p. 135). We can prove things about God, but, as he writes in the *Eight Chapters*, we are unable to attain perfect comprehension of His essence (8, p. 94).

For the *via negativa* to be successful at providing us with a concept that picks out the entity we call God, we need two assumptions. First, the kinds of entities must be finite, for were they infinite, we would never be able to arrive at one entity through a process of elimination. For Maimonides, who believes in a finite universe that is arranged hierarchically, the assumption is a reasonable one. Second, we must have *some* grasp of the meaning of the predicates that we deny of the entity. We cannot prove that God's existence is incorporeal or inanimate, if we have no idea what "corporeal" or "animate" means when denied of God.

But this last point leads to the following familiar objection: If we deny that God is corporeal (and hence we have some grasp of what the term "corporeal" means) then are we not affirming that He is incorporeal, i.e., spiritual? That would be the case if God could only be spiritual or corporeal. But since He is neither, when we deny the one, we are not affirming the other. To explain this Maimonides takes an example from nature: The heavens are composed of an element that is neither heavy nor light; by saying that the heavens are not heavy one cannot infer that they are light. Still, it is *worse* to say of God that He is corporeal than He is spiritual, because corporeal entities are further down in the hierarchy of being than are spiritual entities. Scripture tends to predicate perfections, or what we consider to be perfections, of God.

Maimonides' view that essential attributes must be understood with a negative signification (or else interpreted as actional attributes, when possible), found few defenders among subsequent philosophers. Most thinkers agreed with Aquinas (Thirteenth Century) and Gersonides (Fourteenth Century) that divine attribute-terms signify analogously, i.e., that they mean something analogous when said of God and others. [8] For Gersonides, the claim that attribute-terms signify with "pure equivocation" spells the end of philosophical theology. After all, he argues, if "incorporeal" means something completely different with respect to God, then how can we even claim that God is incorporeal, much less demonstrate it rationally?

More recently, some scholars have claimed that Maimonides' views on negative attributes amount to a "negative theology," which is said to bespeak an agnostic position on the possibility of positive knowledge about God. In other words, we cannot *know* anything about God because we cannot have a direct apprehension of God's essence that will enable us to form a concept of God. But as an interpretation of Maimonides this seems highly unlikely, given that he claims to be able to prove many things about God, and that he does not hesitate to use philosophical descriptions of God like "cause," "intellect," and "necessarily existent," the latter term giving "a clear, unequivocal indication of [God's] essence" (1.61, p. 147).

How Pure is "Pure Equivocation"?

Even Maimonides' claim that attribute-terms signify with "pure equivocation" may be not as radically agnostic as it sounds; it certainly need not support the claims of negative theology. We see from several passages in Maimonides' writings that there can be some *functional resemblance* between things that are signified by equivocal terms. For example, when discussing the faculties of the soul in the *Eight Chapters* Maimonides claims that the term "nutritive" is said equivocally of the nutritive faculty in man, eagle, and donkey, and that the term "sentient" is said equivocally of man and other animals because the souls of different species differ essentially. Nevertheless, he argues, because there is a functional resemblance we can apply the same names. To illustrate this, Maimonides cites as an example the phrase "lit place" when said of three places in which the source of light varies. The phrase is said to signify "with only the name in common" because the cause of the light, as well as its activity, differs in each place. But surely Maimonides does not mean to say that "lit place" *means something entirely different* in each case, at least in our everyday sense of meaning.

Another passage where pure equivocation does not exclude some sort of functional resemblance is found in *Guide* 1.76 (p. 228), where Maimonides claims that the term "body" signifies sublunary and celestial bodies with pure equivocation, since such bodies differ in respect to their essence and true reality. Yet this does not imply that the sublunary and celestial bodies fail to bear some sort of functional resemblance to each other; in fact, both are said to possess dimensionality and to be composed of matter and form. But this resemblance does not require that they are contained within the same species, or even that they agree in some aspect and disagree in another. In other words, Maimonides holds both that there is no resemblance whatsoever between celestial and sublunary bodies and that they are composed of matter and form and possess dimensionality. Of course, the no-resemblance thesis will be stronger in the case of God than in the case of lit places or bodies, but not necessarily strong enough to rule out the sort of functional resemblance we are suggesting here. After all, Maimonides does not create a *new* category of signification to denote terms referring to God and to others ("hyper–equivocation"?), but rather relies on the notion of pure equivocation.

Note that in the example of celestial body Maimonides allows us to apply an essence-designating term to an entity whose essence we do not fully comprehend. We can call the sun a "body" even though we don't fully comprehend the nature of that body. (Remember that according to Maimonides, celestial matter differs essentially from terrestrial matter). If, in order to apply a term to something we required that this thing's essence be fully comprehended, then we would not be justified in saying *anything* about God, or for that matter the celestial bodies, or the separate intellects, since Maimonides believes that we cannot achieve scientific understanding of these entities. Clearly Maimonides feels that this is too strict a requirement for applying names and attributes to God.

On the other hand, if Maimonides holds that pure equivocation, properly understood, excludes even functional resemblance between those things signified by the purely equivocal term, then it is difficult to see what justification he has for applying any term to God, or for that matter, for denying any term of Him. Yet he claims that the philosophers are justified in denying that God has a body, whereas the Kalam incorporealists are not. The latter cannot refute the position that God has a body which is utterly unlike other bodies, because they have no clear notion of what body is. Only the philosophers, who understand that it is the nature of body to be composed of matter and form, can demonstrate that God cannot be a body (1.76, p. 229). By singling out the inadequacies of the Kalam methods, Maimonides implies that other methods, i.e., those of the philosophers, enable us to show that God must be incorporeal with respect to *any* body, even those which differ essentially from each other.

Here we see how critical is the role of philosophy in the purification of our concept of God. Philosophy enables us to acquire and to fine-tune this concept by providing us the means by which we can rule out inadmissible attributes. For example, we can conclusively prove that God cannot have a body of any sort, so clearly terms implying corporeality are inappropriately predicated. Philosophy also enables us to show how putative attribute-terms that appear at first glance to signify different things actually on closer examination signify the same thing and to argue that certain features are essential to God, etc. In short, philosophy teaches us what we can know about God, and teaches us how we should formulate what we know about God. This is no small order.

But philosophy cannot provide us with any *explanatory knowledge* about God, knowledge that tells us what it is about God that makes God what He is. Thus, for example, we can demonstrate that God is an intellect, and that this intellect and its object is the same thing, which is God's essence, but we cannot understand what it is about the divine essence that makes God to be intellect (1.69, pp. 163–166). God is not intellect by virtue of the nature of intellect that he shares with others; rather He is intellect by virtue of His being God. Why this is so is beyond us. What Maimonides emphasizes, therefore, is *not* the unknowability of God but rather His *inexplicability*. God cannot be fully comprehended, despite the fact that we can (indeed, must) learn many things about Him.

The inability to achieve full comprehension is not limited to theology but extends to cosmology as well. There are many things that we can reason about the movements of the heavens, without our having scientific understanding of these movements. We can even reason that these movements are essential to the heavens, but we cannot fully comprehend why the movements that are essential to the heavens are what they are and cannot be otherwise (2.24).

If our interpretation is correct, then Maimonides' theory of divine attribute-terms may not differ so drastically from those of his critics such as Aquinas and Gersonides. The latter, for example, claims that because God's knowledge is (indirectly) the cause of human knowledge, then the term "knower" is said in the strictest or primary sense of God, and by extension, or secondarily, of other knowers.[9] Gersonides assumes that Maimonides rejects such signification. Yet Maimonides nowhere discusses signification "by priority and by posteriority" and there is no direct evidence that he would have rejected it out of hand. True, he does say that divine attribute-terms do not signify "amphibolously" (i.e., ambiguously). That is to say, they do not signify different entities on the basis of a non-essential property that those entities are said to share (1.56, p. 131). But there is no reason to believe that Maimonides understands analogous signification in the same light as amphibolous signification, since his reason for excluding the latter is not relevant for the former. Moreover, as we have just seen, there can be some sort of functional resemblance between things signified by even purely equivocal terms, according to Maimonides.

Summary

Maimonides' theory of divine attributes is intended to purify the believer's concept of God, which has been corrupted by a literalist reading of scripture, the imagination, and the weak and sophistical arguments of the theologians. All people are capable of possessing a concept that genuinely picks out the entity named "God." After only a small amount of philosophical training it is possible to believe that one should negate of God attributes that entail corporeality, potentiality, likeness to creatures, and change (1.35, p. 81) The doctrine that God possesses no likeness to creatures is taught in the Bible, and everyone already is aware of it. But if the believer does not know these doctrines through philosophy, i.e., through the rational demonstrations of their correctness, then she possesses true belief, but not certainty. Without philosophy, the concept of God is vague and unfocused, and can be easily directed away from its referent. Ultimately, what appears to constitute an accurate concept of God, according to Maimonides, is the apprehensions of the intellect about God, which, if arrived at through the process of philosophical demonstration, are certain. However, they are difficult to formulate in language, and, worse, such formulations may be systematically misleading. Philosophy helps us here, too.

Although philosophy fine-tunes for us our concept of God, it does not provide us with scientific knowledge of God's "true reality," His essence. God is unknowable in the sense that His essence is not fully comprehensible or scientifically inexplicable. Like his contemporary Averroes, Maimonides believes that in order to understand the nature of the divine cognition we would have to be God (3.21, p. 485). Only God can fully comprehend God. So the chapters on divine attributes teach us both about the strengths and the weaknesses of philosophy, the religious mandate for the pursuit of scientific knowledge, as well as that knowledge's limitations. Above all, they point out to us the limitations of human language, which means not only verbal speech but mental conceptualization, with reference to God, and provide us with the strategies to circumvent, as much as is humanly possible, those limitations.

Endnotes

[1] For this interpretation see Manekin 1990. For other recent treatments see Stern 1989, Benor 1995, and Seeskin 2001, pp. 43–65.

[2] Cf. *Eight Chapters* 8, pp. 82–83.

[3] See *The Book of Beliefs and Opinions* 2.4, pp. 101–102.

[4] But see 1.57, p. 132, where his formulation ("For all these attributes ["exists," "lives," "is powerful," "knowing"] refer back to one notion in which there is no idea of multiplicity") is reminiscent of Saadiah. That notion, however, cannot be a *property*.

[5] That Moses may have experienced prophecy without the intermediary of an angel suggests a direct relationship; on the other hand, Moses did not achieve knowledge of the divine essence. For these matters see Kreisel 2001, pp. 173 ff. For the question whether the Children of Israel directly experienced God at Sinai, see Ibid., pp. 230–239.

[6] See Seeskin 2000, pp. 30–32 and 182–183. Maimonides does qualify his acceptance of the philosophical characterization of God as cause of the world, because causes necessitate their effects unless there is some impediment, and the world does not proceed necessarily from God. But *pace* Seeskin I don't see what that qualification has to do with his so-called negative theology. And I don't see where Maimonides says that God can be called a cause "loosely," except, of course, in the sense that God can be called anything only "loosely." Here I should point out that Maimonides appeals to "looseness of expression" only with respect to the essential attributes recognized by the Kalam theologians, but not to the philosophers' descriptions of God as "intellect," "ground," "first cause," etc. (1.68,68). Perhaps the reason is that the philosophers, unlike the theologians, understood that God has no essential attributes. But see Lobel 2002, p. 41, for a different reading.

[7] Particularization is the *virtue* of the process of elimination, which Maimonides enthusiastically *recommends* to the reader in 1.59. Through negation one is able "to achieve an apprehension of that which is in our power to apprehend" (p. 139). For an opposing interpretation, see Seeskin 2000, p. 32.

[8] See Broadie 1987 for Aquinas; Wolfson 1977 for Gersonides.

[9] See *The Wars of the Lord* 3.3, pp. 112–115.

4

Creation

Introduction

Maimonides characterizes the view that God created the world out of nothing "a fundamental belief of the Law, second only to belief in the divine unity" (2.13, p. 282). We saw in the previous chapter that the notion of divine unity needs to be explicated through philosophy, and that only philosophy provides us with a conception of God that approximates an apprehension of His true reality. Through philosophy the belief in divine unity is conclusively proven and hence rendered certain. Can philosophy do the same for the creation of the world, i.e., can it provide a conclusive proof that God existed alone and then brought everything else that exists into existence? And if it cannot, is faith in the scriptural tradition the only warrant, or the best one, for believing in creation?

We have seen that Maimonides is quite willing to reinterpret scripture to conform with philosophy when he is convinced of the truth of the latter. In his denial of essential attributes he claims to have the philosophers on his side, for he considers that denial to be self-evident (1.51, p. 112). And even when he takes the trouble to show the reader why God's essence cannot be apprehended, he does not fear that he is treading on controversial ground, for this is a position held by "all men" and "all philosophers."

With respect to creation, however, Maimonides and his philosophical authorities are on opposite sides of the fence. For his most admired authority, Aristotle, held that the world always existed in the way it does now, that it did not come into existence after not existing. Moreover, Aristotle's conclusion seemed to follow inexorably from principles of his science, such as the view that the continual, unending motion of the celestial spheres govern the continual, unending cycle of generation and corruption down below. It seems that to uphold creation Maimonides would have to countenance deviations from basic science, a move that would be extremely difficult for him. Yet, for reasons which we shall examine below, he is deeply committed to upholding creation. Understanding how Maimonides maneuvers in this situation provides valuable insight into his philosophical and religious commitments.

Creation vs. Eternity

Maimonides distinguishes three fundamental positions on the question of the world's origins, attributing them to Moses, Plato, and Aristotle, respectively:

> 1. God "through His will and volition...brought into existence from nothing all the beings as they are, time itself being one of the created things."
> 2. God creates the world, including the heavens, out of pre-existent matter that is coeternal with Him, though on a lower rank.
> 3. God is the eternal cause of the world, which has never ceased to be, nor will cease to be, as it is now (2.13, pp. 281–285).

The first position is sometimes called "creation *ex nihilo* (*min al-adam*)," i.e. out of nonexistence, but that can be misleading: the world is not created out of nonexistence in the way that, say, a table is made out of wood. Maimonides' point is that God creates the form *and* the material substratum of reality. In addition to claiming that the world is created out of nonexistence, he also says that the world is brought into existence "after having been purely and absolutely nonexistent" (p. 281). Following some scholastics, we can call this "creation *post nihilum*." So Maimonides asserts both that the world was created *ex nihilo* and *post nihilum*.[1]

Of course, if time is created together with the world, then what does it mean to say that God exists "before" the world, or that the world exists "after" it was nonexistent? Without time there is no "before" and "after"! Maimonides is aware of the problem, which he attributes to our difficulty in conceiving of time in the context of creation. Our talk of God's preceding the world is based on "a supposition regarding time or an imagining of time and not due to the true reality of time," (p. 280) which is defined as the measure of bodies in motion.

This understanding yields some strange conclusions: God's act of creation is not in time, or even at a time, since time does not exist until the world is created. Paradoxically, it follows for Maimonides that although the world is created, there is no time at which the world does not exist! Maimonides cannot himself avoid speaking of the "endless duration" of God's existence "before" He created the world, a duration that the world does not share. His use of temporal terms to refer to something atemporal is rather confusing.

If Maimonides' exposition here is not very clear, it may be because his concern in this discussion is more theological than scientific. I am not suggesting that the position he defends is philosophically suspect—it appears to me no less coherent than the others—only that he is more interested in the theological implications of his position than its philosophical underpinnings. Note, for example, that the subject of the three aforementioned positions is God, rather than the world. One would have thought that in a discussion of the question of creation Maimonides would have formulated the three positions as:

1'. The world in its entirety is created out of nonexistence after not having existed.
2'. The world is created out of something.
3'. The world is eternal.

But for Maimonides the question of the eternity or createdness of the world hinges upon the conception we have of God's relation to the world. He maintains repeatedly in the *Guide* and later writings that the world is the product of God's will and choice. Only a God who brings the world into existence after having not existed, according to His detailed specifications, can change how the world operates, as in the case of miracles.

As we shall see, Maimonides reads scripture as stating unequivocally that God has power over nature. But he does not dwell on this point now, nor does he emphasize divine will at the outset of the discussion. Perhaps he believed that to do so would damage his case against the philosophers, perhaps even spell the end of science. After all, there is nothing easier than answering "It's God's will" when faced with a scientific problem or a phenomenon that is difficult to explain. Some of the Kalam theologians appealed to God's will to explain *all* phenomena, a move that Maimonides particularly disliked. Still, he himself appeals to God's will when he discusses a series of questions about celestial phenomena. A close examination shows that the appeal to divine will is not intended to provide an alternative explanation, but to rather justify occasions when no scientific explanation is available.

In defending the creation of the world *ex nihilo* Maimonides does not find himself in an enviable position. His "allies" are the very Kalam theologians whose arguments and methodology he belittles. None of the philosophers admired by Maimonides accept creation *ex nihilo*; on the contrary, they find it absurd (3.15, pp. 282–3). Maimonides' strategy will be to transform some of the Kalam proofs into what he considers philosophically respectable, albeit not conclusive, arguments. If the Kalam theologians' errors lay in adopting scientific principles based upon their theological utility, his own starting point will be scientific principles based on the nature of what exists. Since he uses cogent philosophical method to argue the case of religion, this part of the *Guide* is aptly called by Leo Strauss "enlightened Kalam."[2]

Steering Clear of the Kalam Theologians

Most of the Kalam arguments for creation are based on premises that Maimonides rejects. But one premise, arguably the most fundamental one, gives Maimonides pause, and indeed, he will employ a modified version of the premise for his own creation proof. This is what we may call the principle of admissibility (i.e., possibility), concerning which Maimonides writes, "This is not something one hastens to reject in its entirety with nonchalance" (1.73, p. 212). The premise, in its Kalam version, runs something like:

(POA) Whatever can be imagined to exist is admissible.

For example, if I can imagine an elephant flying, or fire freezing, then such phenomena can indeed occur. Only what I cannot imagine, for example, that an elephant is not an elephant, is not admissible.

At first glance this does not seem to be very controversial, since we may say that the notion of fire freezing does not involve a *logical* contradiction; perhaps in some possible world elephants fly and fire freezes. But POA says more than this: it claims that in *this* world it is possible for fire to freeze, because there is nothing in the nature of fire that would prevent it from freezing; indeed, there are no natures that necessitate that a certain thing act or behave in a certain manner. Whereas the world as viewed by the Aristotelians is composed of indeterminate matter and determining form, the world as viewed by Maimonides' Kalam theologians is composed of indeterminate atoms whose properties are, from the standpoint of intellect, arbitrary. Neither nature, nor even the will of God working through nature, determines the way things are. Rather the immediate will of God determines, at every instant, what the world is at that instant. States of affairs have no continuity, nor do things possess causal efficacy. The world is created anew every instant by the inscrutable and arbitrary will of God. There is no nature and therefore no science.

POA is used as a premise in one of the Kalam's methods for proving that the world is created, the method of *particularization*. That method can be described as follows: Whatever exists could be other than what it is (POA). For example, the sun could be bigger or smaller than it is, or in the shape of a cube rather than a sphere. Why, then, is it the way that it is and not in some other way? Because someone or something has particularized, i.e., specified, it to be that way.

Maimonides calls the method of particularization "a most excellent method" of proving the createdness of the world. He himself will employ a version of it in his dispute with the Aristotelians. But he has problems with basing his particularization proof on POA as stated above. As we have just noted, POA's unlimited application would exclude things having natures that determine their behavior. If everything imaginable were admissible, then fish could fly and birds could swim, and nobody could (truthfully) sing, "Fish gotta swim and birds gotta fly." But Maimonides does not want to relinquish the Aristotelian belief that things have natures that determine their behavior.

Moreover, Maimonides considers the imagination to be a "lower" mental faculty shared by us and by other animals. Why allow such a lower faculty to be the arbiter of what is and what is not admissible? Some propositions that cannot be imagined are demonstrably true (e.g., "The distance between hyperbolae and their asymptotes becomes smaller but never disappears") whereas others that can be imagined are demonstrably false ("God has a body") (1.75, p. 210–11).[3] The imagination cannot enable us to determine what may or may not exist.

If the imagination is not the arbiter, according to Maimonides, then what is? Presumably, the intellect. Yet Maimonides realizes that people disagree over what the intellect admits or excludes (p. 211). He himself wonders *how* we determine the difference (in certain cases?) between the intellect and the imagination, or *whether* we can (in certain cases?) appeal to the imagination (3.15, p. 460). We just saw that the notion of creation after nothing relies on a sense of "after" that reflects an "imagining of time rather than the true reality of time." Maimonides acceptance of creation, and the concomitant view that the way the world is could have been otherwise had God chosen it to be so, is responsible for these skeptical considerations about what is admissible, considerations which, as always, Maimonides tries to keep to the minimum required by his insistence on voluntary creation.

To sum up: Maimonides cannot accept POA as stated above, nor the particularization proof based on it. That is because he believes that existent things possess stable natures that determine their behavior. And yet, because he ultimately accepts the idea that the world is a product of the divine will, and could have been otherwise than it is (or, for that matter, not at all), he cannot accept what the philosophers deem to be demonstrably impossible, e.g., creation *ex nihilo* and miracles. His proof will assume a version of POA that he finds compatible with the stable natures of existing things, and with what Aristotle has *demonstrated* to be the explanation of their existence.

Steering Clear of the Philosophers

Having analyzed the other Kalam arguments for creation and found them wanting, Maimonides now takes up the Aristotelian proofs for the eternity of the world. If his worry before was how to preserve the notion of volitional creation without damaging the regnant scientific picture of the world, a picture that he more or less accepted, his concern now is to preserve as much as he can of the Aristotelian worldview without excluding volitional creation. He seems to realize that this is a tall order; at times he sounds almost apologetic when he questions Aristotle's arguments.[4] Maimonides definitely does not want to undermine Aristotelianism as the preeminent scientific theory of the way the world works. What he does want to undermine is a certain *metaphysical and theological conclusion* that had been drawn from Aristotelianism, namely, that God lacks the power to alter or vary the world of which He is First Cause. To do this he maintains that the thesis of the world's eternity is not *entailed* by Aristotle's scientific principles, or at least by his scientific principles worth accepting. By focusing on the issue of the entailment of the world's eternity, he preserves his reader's confidence in the principles themselves. Or to put this another way: Aristotle's principles offer the best scientific explanation we have for the way the world operates, especially, as we shall see, in the sublunary realm. But we must be careful not to draw far-reaching and insufficiently-supported conclusions from those principles.

Maimonides' first step is to argue that the Aristotelians' proofs for eternity are not conclusive but merely probable. In the technical language of the philosophers, they are "dialectical" and not "demonstrative." (2.15, pp. 289–293; in a clever move, Maimonides argues that Aristotle himself did not believe that his arguments for the world's eternity were demonstrative!) This is not to say that the arguments for eternity are wrong or invalid, only that they do not fulfill the conditions of a scientific demonstration laid out by Aristotle himself.[5] Recall that, for Maimonides, a thesis that is conclusively proven trumps all rival contenders for truth, even the plain meaning of scripture. For truth never conflicts with truth, and some truths are capable of rational demonstration. So if the Aristotelians could *demonstrate* that the world is eternal, then "the Law as a whole would become void, and a shift to other opinions would take place" (2.26, p. 330). However, if they are not able to demonstrate the thesis, then Maimonides can rely on religious tradition. (As we shall see, Maimonides also has at his disposal the particularization proof to tip the scales in favor of a volitional creation.)

Maimonides next maintains that the world's creation *post nihilum* is *possible* (in a non-Kalamic sense) and that none of the Aristotelians' arguments conclusively refute the creation thesis. Well, what are some of those arguments? Maimonides divides them into two categories: those whose starting point is the nature of the world, and those whose starting point is the nature of the deity.

Eternity Arguments from the Nature of the World

If we examine the world, says Aristotle, we come to the conclusion that absolute motion, prime matter, and the substance of the celestial spheres are neither generated nor destroyed. If motion, for example, came into being, then it had to be preceded by another motion, and that by another motion; if we want to avoid an infinite regress, we get to a first motion that is itself eternal. According to the Aristotelians, this is the circular motion of the outermost sphere, which is the cause of motion for other motions. All these motions are eternal, so the celestial spheres and their effects are eternal.

Another proof: according to Aristotelian physics, things possessing contrary principles are corruptible; the heavens, not possessing contrary principles (motions), are not corruptible; whatever is not corruptible is not generated; hence, the heavens are not generated, so the world must be eternal.

Arguments like these strike us as unconvincing for many reasons, not the least of which is that we no longer share the scientific picture on which they are based. Indeed, we tend to be somewhat skeptical about the finality of *any* picture of the world, since there have been several scientific revolutions in the course of history. But this is not an option for Maimonides, since he considers that terrestrial science, at any rate, is complete. So rather than attacking the Aristotelian arguments, he takes them down a notch by offering the following skeptical consideration:

Assume that the world was created by God after it did not exist. Isn't it possible that when the world was being created, its nature differed from the nature it was to have after it was completely created, just as the nature of a fetus (breathing, eating, etc.), differs in certain important respects from that of an adult? But if that is the case, then how are we to know for certain that the principles of nature which we derive from our experience of the world after its creation apply to the world beforehand? According to Maimonides, we cannot know this for certain. So when Aristotle attempts to prove, for example, that the heavens are eternal, we have to add to that proof the condition: *"assuming that the world has always been the way it is now"* which at worst begs the question[6] and at best is merely possible. In neither case does the proof fulfill Aristotle's conditions for a demonstration.[7]

Maimonides skeptical consideration about the conformity of the world's order during its creation to its order after its creation is reminiscent of David Hume's skeptical considerations about the conformity of the future to the present. Hume claims in his *Enquiry Concerning Human Understanding* that "all our experimental conclusions proceed upon the supposition that the future will be conformable to the past" (§30), and then he argues that we have no philosophical warrant to conclude that the principle is true. Note that neither Hume nor Maimonides feels that we are not warranted in *practice* to conclude from the present to something which is beyond the present. They give some epistemic weight to probabilistic arguments. (Therein both differ from Kant, who argued that we are *never* warranted to make conclusions about what lies beyond the realm of possible experience.) But both use the argument to take the claims of their opponents (in Maimonides' case, Aristotle; in Hume's case, dogmatic rationalists) down a notch.

There is, of course, an important distinction between the Jewish rabbi and the Scottish philosopher. Hume assumes as a matter of fact that we all expect the future to be like the present; his point is to explain or justify this expectation, given that it is not born of reason. Maimonides does not view our belief that the past was like the present to be a fact about human nature. Since he holds that the world was created after nothing, he argues that it is false. Despite the belief's plausibility, we have grounds to reject it.

Eternity Arguments from the Nature of the Deity

Maimonides defends the creation thesis against three arguments for the world's eternity that are based on God's action, will, and wisdom (2.18, pp. 299–302).

First, if God created the world at a certain time, then before that time He would only be a potential creator, and at that time He would become an actual creator. But there is no potentiality in God, only pure actuality. So the world must be eternal. Maimonides' response is that only material agents move from potentiality to actuality when they act. Non-material agents (of which God is one) can act at one time and not act at another without implying essential change or actualization. He does not provide much of an argument here, and his example of the activity of the active intellect (which is constant, but whose effects may occur at different times because of the preparedness of the recipient) is not entirely apt, as he himself admits. But his purpose is to not to demonstrate that a non-material agent can act at one time and refrain from acting at another, only that this argument of the Aristotelians does not prove this to be impossible.

The argument for eternity from God's will runs as follows: agents will to act, or to refrain from acting, because of incentives and impediments. For example, if I desire a new laptop computer and see a picture of one that fits my budget, I may decide to purchase it when I have the money. The desire and seeing are causes of my decision/volition; my lack of funds is an impediment to my acting on my volition. Now God's will lacks nothing to be implemented, nor is it affected by external causes. So, if God wills the world to be created, it must be created immediately; its creation cannot be delayed. Maimonides' response is to distinguish between a will that is affected by incentives and impediments and God's will, which is not. When God wishes something new to exist, that does not constitute a change in God's essence, since the volition is not due to a cause external to God. Just as God's action can produce different effects at different times without a change in essence, so too can God's will. Unfortunately, Maimonides says little more than this, except to claim that there is no likeness between the will of material and non-material beings.

The third argument states that whatever God's wisdom requires to exist must exist; God's wisdom is eternal, so, the world must also be eternal. Maimonides dismisses this line of argumentation as weak; there is nothing that prevents God's wisdom from requiring that the world have a temporal beginning when it does. Our inability to understand why the world was created *when* it was created is no different from our inability to understand why the world has the number of stars that is does. Both stem from our inability to comprehend fully God's wisdom.

Remember, these responses of Maimonides are not intended to refute Aristotle's arguments for eternity, only to remove them from the category of demonstrations, i.e., conclusive proofs.

Routes Not Taken

As we noted, Maimonides argues that the creation of the world *ex nihilo* and *post nihilum* is a more likely hypothesis than the theory of eternity. Before we take a look at his argument, let us consider two routes that Maimonides could have taken but did not.

Maimonides could have argued that the doctrine of creation can be reconciled with the eternity thesis via the doctrine of *eternal creation*, i.e., that the world either emanates eternally from God (Alfarabi and Avicenna) or that it is an eternal product of an agent (Averroes). This "compatibilist" strategy was certainly familiar to Maimonides from his reading of the Muslim Aristotelians. But he rejects it because of its implications for divine will: If God eternally creates the world, then He is, Maimonides claims, a natural agent rather than a purposive agent. He is bound to create in the way He creates, without will, choice, or purpose. A purposive agent, which brings something into existence after not existing, decides what particular shape that thing will take and is not bound to that shape. Such an agent can will a different shape, if that is what that agent's wisdom requires.

Why not say that God eternally wills the world to be of a particular sort, and since God's will is immutable, the particular sort of world that He wills is immutable? This was the view of Avicenna, and it is probably this view that Maimonides criticizes, when he mentions "one of the recent philosophers" (2.21, p. 314)[8] who claims that God never ceases to will the world to exist. For Maimonides, "never ceases to will" is no different from "wills of necessity": if God always wills the world to exist then God *must* will the world to exist; He has no choice about the matter. And this is not sufficient for Maimonides' conception of voluntary action, for reasons that we shall discuss shortly.

Maimonides could also have argued that because we cannot resolve the question through demonstration, we should accept the fact of creation solely upon the authority of the Biblical prophets. He seems to adopt this view in one passage when he writes, "now inasmuch as this question…is an open question, it should in my opinion be accepted without proof because of prophecy, which explains things to which it is not in the power of speculation to accede" (2.17, p. 294). Since Moses' prophecy teaches that the world was created, there is no need to seek further argument.

But an argument from prophetic tradition, though sufficient, is a last resort for Maimonides. It clearly fails to render belief in the world's creation *certain*, since it rests on accepting the prophetic passages of the Bible as well-attested, and that point may not be granted by the philosophers. (We recall from the chapters on attributes that only rational demonstration provides certainty). But it also fails to ground such belief *rationally*, leaving the thoughtful believer in a state of perplexity and doubt. Coming up with a good argument, even if less than conclusive, is better than relying on a warrant from tradition. And Maimonides apparently believes that his argument for voluntary creation is a good one. It is to that argument we turn now.

The Philosophical Argument for Voluntary Creation

To establish voluntary creation, Maimonides' main argument goes roughly[9] as follows. Say that the world is eternal. This means that it eternally emanates from, or is produced by God in a uniform, stable manner. This uniformity and stability enables it to be an object of scientific knowledge, which, according to Aristotle, is of what is permanent, and not of what is non-essential. But suppose that the world contains phenomena that cannot be explained with reference to the stable nature of things. Suppose, also, that such phenomena cannot be understood as accidental, in the Aristotelian sense that they occur infrequently and without purpose. If such phenomena exist, they could be only be explained as indicative of a divine purpose that cannot be ascertained by humans.

Maimonides claims that he has found examples of such phenomena, e.g., the differing speeds and directions of the motion of the spheres, the number and position of the stars in the spheres, and in general, the diversity of celestial phenomena (2.24, pp. 322–327). He is able to appeal to authorities who question the adequacy of Aristotelian scientific explanation with respect to the heavens. With respect to Aristotle's terrestrial science, says Maimonides, matters are different. There the variety of phenomena is understandable, since sublunary material substances are composed of the four elements (earth, air, fire, and water) in various proportions, which enables these substances to receive a variety of forms. But celestial material substances are composed of one homogeneous matter, which would lead one to expect at the very least a greater uniformity than is the case.

Moreover, Aristotelian physics cannot account for, and indeed conflicts with, basic concepts of Ptolemaic astronomy, a conflict that was well-known to Maimonides' philosophical authorities.[10] This conflict, we are told, is of no consequence to the astronomer, for he makes no existential claims about the system he posits in order to explain the observed movements of the celestial bodies. (2.24, p. 326). But the fact that the heavens are not observed to operate according to the principles of Aristotle's natural science (without a lot of tinkering, anyway) raises serious doubts about the adequacy of Aristotle's theory. Because these celestial phenomena cannot be given a satisfactory natural explanation, and because they do not appear to be random or accidental, Maimonides concludes that they are best attributed to the will of an intelligent deity who particularizes them to be as they are for His own purpose, as His wisdom dictates. This conclusion, Maimonides argues, does not accord well with the eternity of the world thesis. Hence, it is highly probable that the world is created.

Maimonides' argument raises several questions. First, why make the adequacy or inadequacy of Aristotle's celestial science the linchpin of the argument for creation? There were medieval philosophers who were aware of the difficulties with Aristotle's theory yet nevertheless claimed that the world was eternal. Maimonides himself seems to accept much of the Aristotelian picture of the heavens, not just of its observed movements, but of the underlying premises. Second, even if we allow that Aristotle's own explanations are inadequate, does this mean that we have to rule out the possibility that someone else will come up with adequate explanations in the future? In other areas of sciences Maimonides holds that there can be progress. In order to rule out such a possibility in celestial science he has to offer a more general skeptical argument than the one he has offered. And finally, since both the Kalam and Maimonides introduce divine particularization to "explain" natural phenomena, how does his argument for creation differ from theirs?

Maimonides actually addresses the last question, and he as much as concedes that his proof for creation amounts to an argument from particularization. But whereas the Kalam theologians start from divine particularization as a theological assumption, and then construct around it an atomistic ontology to fit their preconceptions, Maimonides arrives at particularization through a consideration of nature and our inability to explain adequately a part of it. He claims that he takes a more empirical approach than the Kalam theologians, since he accepts all that Aristotle has to say in explanation of the sublunary realm, and much of what he has to say in the celestial realm.

But if the approach is truly empirical, then, again, why not allow the possibility that a time may come when science provides an adequate explanation for even the celestial phenomena? Or at least why not leave the matter as a question mark for science? Maimonides does not address these questions. He may have been convinced that science would never adequately explain certain celestial phenomenon because of the limitations of human intellect, which he likes to emphasize in this regard. He nowhere attempts to demonstrate these convictions, and it may be that he was too much the empiricist to do so. In fact, Maimonides was quite correct; the flaws he saw in Aristotelian celestial science could not be overcome within the Aristotelian system.

It is important to see how Maimonides' appeal to divine will and purpose differs from the Kalam's appeal. Unlike the latter it is not intended to *forestall* scientific explanation, or to set the limits of science. I believe that if Maimonides were presented with an alternative, satisfactory explanation of the celestial phenomena, he would accept it. In that case, other phenomena would have to serve as evidence for an unfathomable divine will. And if *no* other evidence could be adduced, then he would lose what he considers to be a good argument for the creation of the world, but nothing more.

Moreover, Maimonides' appeal to divine will does not serve to *explain* the celestial phenomena in question, but to signify that there is no good *natural* explanation. Actually, Maimonides does not appeal to God's inscrutable will or wisdom to *explain* anything. Rather, he suggests that when one accepts the idea that God particularizes the world according to what His wisdom requires, then questions that bother, or have bothered, some scientists are laid to rest. Why are there nine celestial spheres rather than eight? Why does the sublunary matter have the properties that it does? Why are a certain amount of stars in one sphere and not in another? The Aristotelian philosophers feel that they have to come up with some answer, for they believe that natural phenomena have ends or purposes. Neither they nor Maimonides wish to reply with respect to these phenomena, "That's just the way it happens to be."

Finally, unlike the Kalam theologians, Maimonides does not appeal to a divine will that opposes divine wisdom, or is neutral to it. On the contrary, divine will is consequent upon divine wisdom, which is unchanging and, in most cases, fathomable. When Maimonides says that the spheres move in the way they do because God wills them to so move, he means that God's wisdom requires or necessitates that they do (2.22, p. 319; cf. 3.25, p. 505). In other words, there is a good explanation for the spheres to move in the way that they do, only that we do not know it.

Religious Arguments for Voluntary Creation

At the culmination of the chapters on creation, Maimonides maintains that his non-acceptance of the eternity thesis is not because the creation account in scripture compels him to reject it. For if the eternity thesis were proven conclusively—in fact, even if were not—then Maimonides could reinterpret those verses in its light, just as he has reinterpreted the verses that imply divine corporeality. However, since the eternity thesis has not been proven conclusively, then he is free to accept the literal sense of scripture (although, in fact, Maimonides will not accept the literal sense of the creation account itself; rather he accepts the notion presupposed by the literal sense of scripture that the world is the product of divine purpose and choice).

But there is another reason for accepting the creation account: the eternity thesis "as Aristotle understands it," i.e., with the implication that the world proceeds necessarily from a God who cannot modify the customary course of events,

> destroys the Law in its principle, necessarily gives the lie to every miracle, and reduces to inanity all the hopes and threats that the Law has held out, unless—by God!—one interprets the miracles figuratively also, as was done by the Islamic internalists; this, however, would result in some sort of crazy imaginings (2.25, p. 328).

The religious law teaches clearly and repeatedly that God has mastery over nature and can modify it through miracles, and that there is reward and punishment for obedience and disobedience to the Law. Were everything to exist by virtue of natural necessity, then God would be powerless to change nature even in the slightest bit. The deity would no longer be a purposive, intentional agent that *controls* natural causality, but would be subject to it. Such a conception of God and His relationship with the world would annul "all the external meanings of the Law with regard to which no intelligent man has any doubt that they are to be taken in their external meaning" (p. 329). And since Maimonides accepts the Law without question as a source of truth, he accepts it as evidence for the world being the product of a volitional agent.

With these remarks Maimonides seems at first glance to have returned to the conception of a personal deity who intervenes miraculously into the natural order of things, and responds with rewards and punishments to those who obey and disobey Him. Doesn't that go against the naturalistic interpretation of reward and punishment that we mentioned in the previous chapter, and that we will see developed in the next? For that matter, why in the midst of a philosophical discussion does Maimonides talk about the *religious* consequences of the eternity thesis? Isn't that somewhat of an intellectual cop-out?

Some scholars have suggested that Maimonides' message here is political rather than philosophical. His overt rejection of the eternity thesis is really the result of that thesis's effect on the multitude, who need faith in miracles and supernatural rewards and punishments in order to motivate their own virtuous behavior. The eternity thesis "destroys the Law in its principle" *for the common people* since they are not capable of conceiving divine reward and punishment without the notion of a personal God who intervenes into nature.[11] According to some of these scholars, Maimonides secretly accepts the eternity thesis, and, in this chapter, hints to his students about why he apparently adopted the opposing view.

Yet it is possible to interpret Maimonides' views on miracles and reward and punishment without having to posit a wholly personal deity, and without having to obliterate the distinction between the natural and the supernatural. If such an interpretation, which we shall present in the next chapter, is correct, then we have removed an important argument for reading Maimonides' "esoterically."

As for the legitimacy of Maimonides' appeal to scripture in the midst of a philosophical argument, that depends on what we mean by "appeal to scripture." Maimonides does not say that the doctrine of creation must be accepted because we must accept the literal meaning of scripture in all cases. For when scripture clashes with demonstrated truth, "the gates of figurative interpretation" are open, and a non-literal interpretation can be offered, as we saw in the last chapter. As we noted above, had he been forced to conclude that the world was eternal, he could have interpreted scripture to fit that thesis. But Maimonides believes that there are times *when the gates of figurative interpretation are shut.* There are passages whose external meaning can be doubted by "no intelligent man." Maimonides holds that the religious law clearly presupposes that God is a volitional rather than a natural agent, and, specifically, that God works miracles, however the actual working of miracles is to be understood.

Summary

According to Maimonides, the question of the world's temporal creation vs. its eternity is not decidable on purely scientific grounds. We can give no conclusive proof, physical or metaphysical. Because we have no conclusive proof, we are, in principle, free to choose what appears to us to be the most reasonable. But there are theological implications of both theses. If the world is eternal, then it is not the product of a purposive agent who particularizes it in a certain way. This entails that much of what the Law teaches as fundamental is false or meaningless. If the world is created, i.e., particularized by God to exist after absolute nonexistence (in some non-temporal sense of "after"!), then

God has mastery over nature, and much of what the Law teaches as fundamental makes sense.

Since Maimonides believes that the Law is a source of truth, he is motivated to accept what the Law presupposes, namely, a purposive deity. Since he is a thinking man of the Twelfth Century, he wishes to ground creation rationally. His method is to take what he considers the strongest argument for creation, the Kalam particularization argument, and to make it philosophically respectable by basing the argument on the way things are. Specifically, he argues that there are anomalies in the celestial sphere that cannot be satisfactorily explained by (Aristotelian) science. Since they are stable features of world, their existence cannot be accidental or without a purpose, and hence their cause of existence is the inscrutable will of God, which is consequent upon His wisdom. One might say that the inexplicable celestial anomalies serve the same purpose as miracles; both cannot be accounted for in terms of natural (i.e., Aristotelian) science. But only the latter involves a violation of the customary course of events, as we shall presently see.

Endnotes

[1] Cf. Seeskin 2000, 71–77.

[2] Strauss 1952, p. 41.

[3] See Freudenthal 2000.

[4] Cf. 2.22, p. 320: "Do not criticize me for having set out the doubts that attach to [Aristotle's] opinion."

[5] This is how I understand "render void the proofs" towards the end of 2.17, p. 294.

[6] Josef Stern called my attention to this.

[7] I have condensed the discussion here almost beyond recognition; Maimonides uses these skeptical considerations to show the possibility of creation, i.e., by showing that Aristotle's arguments against creation are probable.

[8] Translating *ba'da* as "one" rather than "some"; see p. 314, n. 1.

[9] For a more precise interpretation, see Davidson 1987.

[10] See Langermann 1991.

[11] On the political/pedagogic reading see Kreisel 1999, p. 220.

5

Divine Governance and Providence

Introduction

The conception of God that emerges from the Hebrew Bible is that of a person who enters into covenants with individuals and peoples, gives laws, rewards the obedient and punishes the rebellious. By contrast, the conception of God that emerges from the Aristotelian philosophers is that of an unmoved prime mover and/or first cause, whose nature is intellect and whose activity is contemplation, and who does not enter into any direct relation with the world, and is certainly unaffected by it. The attempt to harmonize these conceptions had already started in late antiquity (even earlier, if one considers philosophical interpretations of Greek myths), and by the time of Maimonides, the Muslim philosophers had provided the framework and many of the details for a philosophical interpretation of how God governs the world. The general strategy was to transfer to intermediaries many of the functions that the Bible had initially assigned to God, just as the absolute powers of a monarch are often transferred to institutions: governmental, legal and other. God was said to govern the world through the celestial bodies and incorporeal intelligences, which implant *natures* in the existents of the sublunary world that control and preserve them. On this scheme (developed by the Aristotelian commentator, Alexander of Aphrodisias, fl. 200 AD) divine providence is limited to this governance, i.e., to that which nature necessitates (Cf. 3.17, p. 464).

Of course, the Bible itself often posits intermediaries that influence the world below, such as the celestial bodies, and this allows

Maimonides to claim that the Bible and the philosophers agree that divine governance is through the medium of these celestial intermediaries (2.5, pp. 260–1). According to Maimonides there seems to be little disagreement between the philosophers and the Bible on the question of divine governance. The only point of divergence pertains to the Biblical teaching of phenomena such as miracles, and certain divine rewards and punishments. Even prophecy can be accounted for by the philosophers, although perhaps not as the Bible envisions it.

In this chapter we shall consider certain phenomena that are traditionally attributed to the intervention into the natural order of a personal God, such as prophecy, revelation, providence, and reward and punishment, and see how they are given a philosophical interpretation by Maimonides. This interpretation is consistent with the depersonalization of God that we saw in chapter 2, but also with the emphasis on divine will that we saw in chapter 3. For the personal/impersonal distinction is not the same as the voluntary/natural distinction, and an impersonal god need not be subject to nature, even to its own nature. The reason we tend to conflate the distinctions is that we sometimes think only of persons as possessing free will, which implies, according to one common interpretation, that their will is not subject to natural causality. The Bible certainly conceives of God as a person who can, if He likes, directly act within history and overcome nature (or whatever is recognized by Biblical authors as "nature"). But God, according to Maimonides, does not "intervene" or "respond," if that implies being affected by something. Nor does He have other characteristics which we nowadays associate with persons, such as sensations, memory, and all that which is connected to bodies. True, God, like the incorporeal intelligences, is said to have intellect, will, and intention, although these words mean something very different for Him than for us.[1]

God is not a natural agent because His effects do not proceed necessarily from Him, as, for example, the sunlight from the sun. Actually, for Maimonides it is incorrect to posit a distinction, much less an opposition, between the divine and the natural. For, as we have noted, Maimonides understands "natural actions" as God's "ways" or "actions" (3.32, 525)[1] and the "stable nature of things" as decreed by God's eternal will. So rather than ask whether God has mastery over nature we can ask whether God can will what appears to be a change in His actions, actions that are also determined by His will, consequent upon His wisdom. And as we have seen, Maimonides answers this question in the affirmative.

Of course, talk of divine "will" and "actions" should remind us that descriptions of God are approximate at best and misleading at worst. They represent ways in which we try to refer to an entity that cannot be fully comprehended. So we should be careful lest we mistake divine "will," "wisdom," 'intellect," etc. as *positive attributes*. Scripture and philosophy enable us to learn things about God, e.g., that He governs for the most part through the stable nature of what exists. But both also teach us not to make claims about God's essence.

Prophecy

In the Hebrew Bible the deity communicates to people in various ways, the most common of which is prophecy. A prophet receives the communication from God in a vision or in a dream and then acts upon the communication, or transmits it to others. Prophecy is often, though not necessarily, concerned with predictions; the Biblical prophets usually use predictions in order to harangue their listeners about present evils ("Repent before it's too late!") While their message often seems the same, the prophets of the Bible themselves do not appear to have much in common. They come from different backgrounds and classes, and are called to prophesy at various stages of their life. At times they appear to be randomly chosen vehicles of the divine message, appearing with no special qualification, although most possess moral virtues and rhetorical skills.

This picture of prophet and prophecy was familiar to the Muslim philosophers primarily from the Qur'an, as well as other traditional writings.[2] As scientists/philosophers they offered a naturalistic explanation of prophecy that compelled them to reinterpret the sacred texts of their tradition, even if these explanations seemed to fly in the face of tradition. For example, they argued that only a mature individual who had perfected his intellect, and who was able to achieve the level of concentration necessary to receive the divine message, could be a prophet, despite the fact that some prophets in the Qur'an appeared to be unlearned.

Since the Muslim Aristotelians considered prophets to be as wise and learned in the sciences as philosophers, much space was devoted to the question of what distinguished one from the other. Some held that prophets were able to grasp truths in a non-discursive, intuitive act; others, that they were able to achieve knowledge beyond that of even the greatest philosophers. Still others, especially Alfarabi, emphasized the role played by the prophet's imagination in translating the pure intellectual communication into parables and images, and even laws, that the multitude could understand, a point to which we shall return. In Alfarabi's system, the prophet was identified both with the priest

(Imam) and the Platonic philosopher-king, who legislates and governs the virtuous society.[3]

The requirement that the prophet possess a perfected intellect went against the plain sense of the Qur'an and the Bible, but it was an important element in the naturalization of prophecy. For now the phenomenon of prophecy could be interpreted as an emanation or overflow of eternal truths from the supernal intelligence, the active intellect, to the prophet, occurring whenever the conditions were ripe. The nature and significance of a particular prophetic message were a function of the circumstances, natural and historical, in which prophets found themselves. According to some Muslim philosophers, the prophets received general, eternally true principles, which they then applied to the particular case at hand (hence the importance of the imagination, which particularizes the universal truths). We can think of the prophet, on this model, as similar to today's highly skilled science writer, who intuitively grasps a complex physical theory, unpacks its various components, and then communicates it to the public at large, using examples and analogies from daily life. We say of such a writer that he has a remarkable gift for explaining difficult concepts. But we do not have to posit the existence of a personal God who sends him the latest scientific development directly, or via a winged angel!

Maimonides was very much drawn to the naturalist interpretation of prophecy.[4] He defines prophecy as "an overflow overflowing from God, may He be cherished and honored, through the intermediation of the active intellect, toward the rational faculty in the first place and thereafter toward the imaginative faculty" (2.36, p. 369). The act of prophesying does not result from a discrete, personal communication addressed directly to the individual by the deity. Rather the flow of knowledge from God to the active intellect and beyond is continuous: when the conditions are ripe, the prophet will receive the message, just as a listener receives information by tuning into a television station that broadcasts its programs continually. Pushing the analogy further (as is often done with this particular analogy), one can say that just as the particular quality of the broadcast will vary according to the quality of the television receiver, its loudspeakers, atmospheric conditions, etc. so too the particular quality and even import of the message will vary according to the natural capacity of the prophet to receive the message, her state of mind at the time of the communication, her talent in communicating the message to her audience, and the circumstances in which she finds herself. Because the intellectual "overflow" reaches the imaginative faculty the prophets generally grasp eternal truths as parables.

Maimonides also claims that all prophets save Moses prophesized when asleep, or in a trance (*Introduction to Helek*, p. 419). This point is important because it allows him to make the rather striking claim that all the Biblical prophecies were received as dreams and visions, even when the Bible does not explicitly say so. Moreover, he holds that wherever the Bible mentions that an angel was seen or heard, this must have been in a prophetic vision or a dream. So the Biblical story of Jacob's wrestling with the angel (Genesis 32:23–33), for example, took place only in Jacob's mind, according to Maimonides. Later Biblical commentators raised various difficulties over this exegetical move, e.g., if Jacob only dreamed that he wrestled with an angel, then how could he have acquired a permanent limp as a result of the encounter? (One answer given by Gersonides: he hurt his foot when he thrashed about in his dream!)

One can say with a certain amount of exaggeration that Maimonides was one of the first rabbinic Jews to read certain Biblical stories as psycho-dramas that occur within the mind of the prophet. Some other Biblical stories, such as the story of the Garden of Eden, or the book of Job, are read by Maimonides as straight parables. The stories appear in the Bible because they are allegories for eternal truths.

For Maimonides, what makes certain knowledge *prophetic* has to do with the nature of the individual that receives the divine communication rather than with the nature of the divine communication itself; more precisely: the nature of the individual prophet determines how he receives that communication. When individuals are such that they are able to receive the intellectual overflow from the active intellect to their own intellect, and then from their intellect to their imaginative faculty, then they are prophets. Individuals who only receive the overflow to their intellects are philosophers, whereas individuals who only receive the overflow to their imaginations are rulers and diviners (2.37, p. 374). The prophet combines theoretical, practical (i.e. ,political), and divinatory perfections in varying degrees. This is why prophets are the ideal rulers, Maimonides' own adaptation of Alfarabi's interpretation of Plato's philosopher-king.

Although deeply influenced by the naturalist interpretation of prophecy advocated by Muslim Aristotelians like Alfarabi,[5] Maimonides parts company with them on at least two points: first, he claims that even when the natural conditions for prophecy have been fulfilled, the prophet will not prophesy unless God wills it. Were prophecy to proceed from God necessarily upon the fulfillment of the natural conditions, that would make God a natural rather than a volitional agent, subject to the control of the prophet. But according to the Bible and the rabbis, God turns "whom He wills, whenever He wills it into a prophet—but only someone perfect and superior to the utmost degree" (2.32, p. 362). In other words, when the natural conditions are met, God's will is still required to empower the prophet to receive prophecy.

There is no need to interpret this requirement as assuming the sort of personal, interventionist God that Maimonides consistently treats metaphorically. For Maimonides never writes that God's *personal intervention* in nature is necessary for the occurrence of prophecy, only that His *will* is. And this will is likely to be identified by him with God's "eternal will," which is constant and unchanging (cf. 1.10, p. 36; 3.17, p. 469). What Maimonides opposes is the attempt to reduce divine prophetic activity to the level of *natural necessity*. And he opposes this for the same reason that he opposes the eternity thesis: namely, the implication that God cannot suspend the nature of things. So God can *prevent*, should He so wish, a prophet from prophesying, even if he is fully prepared to receive the prophetic overflow. The prevention of prophecy is "like all the miracles and takes the same course as they" (2.32, p. 361).[6]

The second significant difference between Maimonides and the Muslim philosophers lies in his recognition of a *sui generis* form of prophecy that is *legislative* in nature, Moses' prophecy. Now, the Muslim philosophers did not deny that prophecy may produce law. Alfarabi, for example, held that prophets convert their prophecy into laws just as they convert it into images and parables. But this conversion, which is a conscious activity of the prophet, produces an *imitation* of the pure prophetic message. Maimonides also did not deny that some prophets other than Moses may grasp certain truths and use arguments to teach those truths to others. They may even grasp that some activities are divinely mandated, permitted or forbidden. For example, once the belief in one God is demonstrated to be true, it follows that it is wrong (both mistaken and fruitless) to worship other gods. Through prophetic revelation Abraham is informed that he and his progeny are mandated to undergo circumcision. But this revelation is not the same as the revelation that is by nature legislative for an entire people. Only Moses' prophecy (i.e., the Pentateuch) expressly called the people to obey certain laws, and that prophecy itself announces that those laws will never be abrogated (2.39).

Maimonides never explains *why* only Moses' prophecy is legislative in nature, and it may be that no such answer is possible, given that he holds that the true reality of Mosaic prophecy cannot be understood. He does argue that no other divine law is possible because the law of Moses is perfect and there can be only one model of perfection for any species (2.39, p. 380) He also holds that the overflow of knowledge can be so abundant as to compel a prophet to prophesy to others. Since Moses achieved the greatest apprehension of divine governance possible for any mortal, it is plausible that his prophecy would set out the governance of all humans, Jews and non-Jews alike; the former via the Mosaic law, the latter via the Noahide laws, i.e. those laws which, according to rabbinic Judaism, are binding on gentiles. In one passage in the *Commentary on the Mishnah* Maimonides suggests that Moses attained the level of the "angelic," i.e., the separate celestial intelligences (*Introduction to Helek*, p. 419). Perhaps this means that Moses apprehends eternal truths which he then translates into eternal laws. But Maimonides is silent on this issue.

One final point: Maimonides insists in the *Code of Law* that the real author of the Mosaic Law is God, and that none of it was written by Moses "on the basis of his own opinion" (*Repentance* 3:8, p. 84b).[7] In the *Commentary on the Mishnah* he conjures up the rabbinic image of Moses faithfully transcribing God's speech (*Introduction to Helek*, p. 420), although he notes in the same place that 'speech' should understood metaphorically; only Moses knew how he received the prophecy. In *Guide* 2.28 Maimonides makes clear that terms such as "say," "send," "speak," and "call" are to be taken as metaphors when used with reference to God (p. 410).

Moreover, there is nothing in Maimonides' writings that rules out the possibility that Moses' prophetic message, consisting of eternal truths and imperatives, was adapted to his historical circumstances through the filter of his practical reason and imaginative faculty— provided that in that filtering Moses added nothing to that message "on the basis of his own opinion." If I may use a flawed analogy: the mere fact that Aristotle's logic was expressed first in Greek did not make logic Aristotle's own opinion, not, at least according to Kant, who considered it to be universally and necessarily true. Maimonides would probably admit that there is translation from universal truth to law and historical narrative, even to laws that are most pertinent in concrete circumstances. What he denies is that anything in the Law bears the stamp of Moses' individual (i.e., non-angelic!) personality. The Law is what God gave to the ancient Hebrews, taking into account, among other things, their historical and cultural circumstances. Or to put this differently: had some one else achieved the angelic rank, and not Moses, at that time and historical circumstance, then presumably the resultant Law would be no different.

Governance and Providence

We began this chapter by contrasting the Biblical conception of a personal God who creates and provides for the world, one who comes into contact with humans, with the Aristotelian conception of a remote, impersonal deity whose entire activity consists of self-intellection. The medieval Jewish philosophical discussion of divine providence is often portrayed as an attempt to synthesize these two conceptions. Yet this does not do justice to either the implicit naturalism of much of the Biblical account (God often lets things run their course) or to the various interpretations of divine providence within Greek philosophy. Moreover, it conflates the issue of the *extent* of divine providence, i.e., what phenomena fall under the range of providential activities, and its *mechanism*, i.e., how providence works. These two issues should be kept distinct. You can claim that every single event is a result of divine activity, and at the same time be a thoroughgoing naturalist. All you have to do is to make natural processes the vehicle for God's activity (or even better: to identify some of God's actions with the natures of things).

Maimonides agrees with the Muslim philosophers that God's activity is eternal and His essence immutable, and that God does not *respond* to events. He also agrees with them that God governs or supervises the world via intermediaries, e.g., the celestial spheres, intellects, and in general, the natures of things. And, finally, he holds that Biblical descriptions characterizing God as a person are to be interpreted metaphorically. These three assumptions are enough to rule out both literal Biblical conceptions of a personal God who *intervenes* in history, and deist conceptions of a God whose activity is limited to the creation of an autonomous, mechanistic system of nature.

Where he differs is over the extent of divine providence, or better, what providential significance, if any, should be accorded to various phenomena. To make everything the result of *direct* divine causal activity, or to overly restrict its sphere, are both unacceptable. Maimonides stakes out a middle position that reflects the Biblical conception of a God who provides in a general way for all of creation, but who also provides specifically for some individuals and peoples.

General and Individual Protection from Material Evils

God governs and provides for all of creatures through natural causes, i.e., through the specific natures implanted them as members of a species. Humans, like other animals, possess psychic and bodily faculties that enable them to survive for a certain life span and to reproduce, thus ensuring the survival of the species. Unique to humans is a faculty that "according to the level of the perfection of the individual in question, governs, thinks, and reflects on what may render possible the durability of himself as an individual and the preservation of his species" (3.17, p. 465). This, of course, is the intellect, specifically that part of the intellect which is concerned with the individual's survival. Let us call this the "survival-calculating intellect" and note that Maimonides considers it to be part of the *governance*, i.e., general providence of the world.

In addition to this sort of general or species-related providence, Maimonides recognizes that some humans enjoy greater prosperity than others, and to account for at least some of these cases he posits "individual providence" (3.17, p. 472). This sort of providence is restricted by him to human individuals and made a function of the degree of divine overflow of truths to the individual, or what we may call his or her *intellectual achievement* or *perfection*. Since there are varying degrees of intellectual achievement, there will be varying degrees of individual providence.

But what is the connection between individual providence, material goods, and intellectual perfection?[8] Some have interpreted Maimonides as saying that individual providence is nothing more than the longer, healthier, and more prosperous life lived by the wise man than by the fool, all things being equal. Knowledge of the world and the way it works (derived ultimately from God via the active intellect) helps to *protect* humans from material evils, and *provide* them with material goods, to varying extents.

Yet there are difficulties with this interpretation. For one thing mere knowledge is not enough to affect one's behavior and its outcome. I may have learned a lot about tobacco and lung cancer and still smoke. So why should intellectual perfection be sufficient for individual providence? Moreover, on this interpretation, the intellect that is perfected appears to be the "survival-calculating" sort. If I refrain from smoking cigarettes because I have been convinced that they are dangerous to my health, then although I am acting above the level of base instinct, my concern is still with physical survival. If this is correct, then the distinction between general and individual providence becomes one of degree rather than of kind.

Others have interpreted Maimonides as saying that the wise man *ipso facto* achieves a higher reward than the fool, regardless of his material fortunes. That is because human happiness depends ultimately on the perfection of the theoretical intellect. Here the difference between general and intellectual providence is pronounced; the former concerns material goods and evils whereas the latter, spiritual. The difficulty with this interpretation is that Maimonides implies very strongly that those who enjoy great degrees of individual providence are rewarded with *material* goods and are protected from *material* evils.

What these two interpretations share in common is an unwillingness to make material goods and evils dependent upon intellectual perfection, where the intellect involved is other than survival-calculating. For there does not seem to be any natural connection between the perfection of the theoretical intellect and material prosperity. Yet, according to Maimonides, the Bible provides us with conclusive evidence for such a connection: "All the stories figuring [in scripture] concerning *Abraham* and *Isaac* and *Jacob* are an absolute proof of there being individual providence" (3.17, p. 472). These were men who achieved perfection of the theoretical intellect and enjoyed material prosperity.

It seems that once the Biblical stories convince Maimonides of the phenomena of individual providence, he does his best to connect it with a stable process such as the overflow of the divine intellect from the active intellect to the prophets and the righteous: "For it is this measure of the overflow of the divine intellect that makes the prophets speak, guides the actions of righteous men, and perfects the knowledge of excellent men with regard to what they know" (3.18, p. 475). As we shall see below, Maimonides holds that material perfection is a necessary condition for intellectual perfection, which implies that the latter carries with it the former. It is possible to understand the individual providence spoken of here as the possession of material goods and the lack of material defects that *accompanies* intellectual perfection. But how does this work?

Perhaps one can compare the state of these superior humans to that of the celestial spheres: the measure of intellectual overflow that accrues to the latter is reflected in the excellence of the celestial matter, which is not subject to change or to harm. Likewise, a prophet or a righteous person who has achieved an excellent mind also possesses an excellent (non-rational) soul and body that ensures his well-being and prosperity. This is an interesting way to make sense of Maimonides, but he himself does not make the comparison. On the contrary, we recall that Moses, the greatest prophet, is said to have achieved the level of the angelic, the separate intellects that are *devoid* of matter. This seems to indicate that the intellectual overflow may result in the "decorporealization" of humans, as much as is humanly possible.

This leads to a second possible answer to the question of how intellectual perfection protects someone from material evils: insofar as righteous people are connected with God, they have ceased to a large degree to be corporeal, and so *material evils do not affect them.* The case of this *in extremis* is that of the prophets Moses, Aaron, and Miriam (3.51, p. 627). They achieved such a level of apprehension and love of God, their soul was in such a state of intellectual pleasure, that their death was a blessing rather than a curse, because their release from corporeal existence was then made permanent. As for those not on this level of Moses, Miriam, and Aaron, they are unaffected by material ills when they are in a state of communion with God. When they are affected by material ills they are no longer in that state of communion, but are left to nature, chance, and their own devices, as we shall shortly see.

Divine Recompense

Once Maimonides has interpreted individual providence along impersonalistic lines, i.e., as a function of the divine intellectual overflow, he is able to interpret divine reward and punishment accordingly: the world is created such that the consequences of acting wisely and prudently are a long and healthy life; this is what the Bible understands by "divine reward." Similarly, if one lives foolishly and barbarously one becomes subject to the many ills that afflict the body, and this is what the Bible understands as "divine punishment." We saw in chapter 2 that Maimonides views the destruction of the Biblical cities of Sodom and Gomorrah to be in accordance with God's eternal will, i.e., the way the world operates. There is no need to picture God as a personal judge intervening within nature, since nature itself is identified with some of God's actions. On this model divine reward and punishment are built into the stable nature of what exists.

Of course, we already know that divine recompense is not *only* built into the stable nature of what exists, for God occasionally rewards and punishes miraculously (2.25, p. 328). For example, according to the Bible, God promises Israel that if they observe His statutes, the rain will fall at the proper times. There is certainly nothing in natural science that connects the falling of rain with the performance of divine commandments (unless there are commandments to seed clouds!) In his *Essay on Resurrection*, Maimonides is very explicit:

> The Torah affirms it as a continuous miracle over the generations, that is, success in [Israel's] activities if they obey God, and failure if they disobey...their success and failure are not the result of

natural causes or customary existence, but are linked to their obedience and disobedience....They are singled out by this great miracle: success or failure in their activities will always be linked to their actions (*Resurrection*, p. 231).

So while all humans are rewarded or punished naturally according to their actions (cf. 3.17, p. 471), only Israel, it appears, has miracles performed on its behalf as part of divine recompense. Once again, this does not imply divine intervention but only the occurrence of certain non-natural phenomena according to the divine will.

The Question of Desert

Of course, if divine recompense is to be just, it is not enough to reward and punish people according to their actions; their reward and punishment must be *deserved*. But this raises a difficulty with the notion that God builds reward and punishment into the system of nature. For nature does not discriminate with its actions: a flood sweeps the righteous away with the wicked. And if we equate the customary natures of things with God's "ways" or "actions," as Maimonides is generally understood to do, then it appears that God Himself is the cause of undeserved evil. But how can He then be just?

The question of divine justice is at the heart of *Guide* 3.17, a notoriously difficult chapter to grasp. Maimonides begins by summarizing five views on divine providence:

1. There is no divine providence, or for that matter, a God who knows the world; all worldly phenomena are chance and accidental (the view of Epicurus).

2. God's knowledge and providence does not extend to the individual, although providence extends to the species. Hence, the non-essential properties of individuals are chance and accidental and have no providential significance (the view of Aristotle).

3. God wills directly all sublunary phenomena; there is nothing chance and accidental. God is omniscient. Humans have no ability to act; what God wills is *ipso facto* just (the view of the Asharite Kalam).

4. Humans have the ability to act. God is omniscient. All sublunary events are in accord with divine wisdom, and all creatures are justly recompensed. There is nothing chance and accidental (the view of the Mutazilite Kalam).

5. Humans have the ability to act. God is omniscient and just. All recompense is deserved, though we are ignorant of the modes of

desert (the view of "the Law [=Torah], according to the multitude of our scholars").

As you can see, each of these positions contains several variables, which makes their analysis tricky. We discuss the question of divine omniscience in the section after the next one; let us focus now on the question of desert.

Maimonides implies that only the fifth position takes the question of desert seriously. Only "the Law, according to the majority of scholars," truly teaches that "All *God's ways are judgment*" And Maimonides agrees in 3.17 that everything that happens to somebody is deserved. So it is a bit surprising when he presents his own position as varying somewhat from 5:

> 5'. Individual providence and divine recompense are consequent upon the divine intellectual overflow to humans. All recompense is deserved, but we cannot see how, because of our ignorance of the manner of divine providence (Maimonides' own position).

What distinguishes 5' from 5 is the emphasis on the presence of intellect as a necessary condition of the appropriateness and deservedness of recompense, and the shift of the locus of our ignorance from the "modes of desert" to the manner of divine providence.

To understand this distinction, consider Maimonides' own example of an "accidental evil"— the drowning of "excellent and superior men" when a hurricane sinks their ship (3.17, pp. 465–6). According to the different opinions on providence,

> 1. & 2. The drowning was accidental and undeserved. (Epicurus and Aristotle).
> 3. The drowning was undeserved and the result of divine will. (Asharites).
> 4. The drowning was undeserved, but it provides the good people with a reward in the afterlife (Mutazilites).
> 5. The drowning was deserved, but we cannot fathom the various modes of desert (the Law, according to the multitude of scholars).

And according to Maimonides' view,

> 5'. The drowning was deserved, because the men decided to board the ship, but we cannot fathom God's governance.

As Maimonides puts it, "the fact that the people in the ship went on board…is, according to our opinion, not due to chance, but to divine will in accordance with the deserts of those people as determined in His judgments, the rule of which cannot be attained by our intellects (3.17, p. 472)."

From the standpoint of nature, the drowning of the excellent men is an accident; yet in some unfathomed way their fate is deserved because it is partly a consequence of their decision to go on board the ship.

This is *not* to say that the men drowned because they were sinful or guilty in some unknown way. Maimonides attributes that line of thinking to Job's friend Eliphaz, identifies it with the view of the Law "according to the majority of scholars" (3.23, p. 494) and thinks that the Book of Job repudiates it (p. 493). Nor is Maimonides saying that the men deserved their death because of lapses of judgment, because they should have known, for example, that there would be a hurricane, or that it was foolish to travel in a ship during the hurricane, etc. Reasons of these sorts focus on pedestrian examples of our ignorance, and while they explain to us why the men died, they do not explain to us why their death was *deserved*.

Maimonides' point is much deeper. Although we can understand much about divine governance in the world—indeed, the natural sciences examine God's ways in the world, and that examination is mandated by the Law—we cannot understand how individual deserts play a role in the natural determination of events willed by God. Once again, we can prove that God is just and hence that accidents are deserved, but we cannot know very much about the "how" or "why" of providence.

No Room for Desert?

At the end of the *Guide* (3.51) Maimonides returns to the question of accidental suffering, this time without mentioning desert at all. He writes that as long as an individual with perfect knowledge is meditating about God, that individual is protected from all evils, including material. When she is distracted and abandons God, she is left to the vagaries of chance, which likely includes what we have called accidental suffering. The second part of this sounds thoroughly compatible with the Aristotelian explanation of the shipwreck above as accidental and undeserved and provides Maimonides with a second solution to the problem of accidental suffering. But it is hard to square with his first solution, unless he thinks that being left to the vagaries of chance is *deserved*. This produces strange results. Say, for example, you interrupt your meditation about God when the telephone rings. Distracted, you pick up the phone and hear your broker telling you that you have lost money in the stock market, which saddens you greatly. It seems odd to say that you *deserved* to be sad because you answered the phone (and broke your communion with the deity!) At best we may say that you are *responsible* for abandoning yourself to the vagaries of chance, and for letting yourself be affected by them.

But maybe it is not so odd, if Maimonides holds that God's providence is partly incomprehensible. You do not deserve to be sad *because* you answered the phone any more than you deserve to be happy because your stocks have gone up. But insofar as your actions are the result of thought, the notions of providence and recompense, and desert, are connected. One of the things that distinguishes material and spiritual recompense is the apparent lack of order in the former compared with the order in the latter. There is nothing accidental in the attainment of spiritual good (although there is something accidental in the opportunities for such attainment). The more one learns of eternal truths, for example, the more one benefits from spiritual recompense when contemplating them; it is as predictable as that. To be left to the vagaries of chance means that there is little apparent rhyme or reason to winning the lottery or being hit by a truck. But since all God's ways are judgment, and since God is omniscient, there must be *some* explanation to the deservedness of what happens to us *qua* thinking individuals.

Perhaps we can harmonize the two treatments of accidental evil (in 3.17 and 3.51) by saying that Maimonides is talking about different cases. In the case of the drowning, the evil results in part from the "excellent men's" *deliberate* action of boarding the ship; this makes the question of desert *appropriate* (although the actual consequence is incomprehensible). In the case of the interruption of the bond between God and humans (as when the phone rings), the reaction to the phone is not a deliberate action; any animal would do the same. In that case we have returned to the realm of general providence, in which there is no distinction between animals and humans, and the question of desert is irrelevant.

Miracles

We saw above that Maimonides believes in miracles because of scriptural passages that resist metaphorical explanation. But if such passages could be explained convincingly as metaphors, then he would be inclined to do so. This emerges from the following passage in the *Essay on Resurrection*, which captures both his acceptance and devaluation of miracles in a nutshell:

> My endeavor, and that of the select keen-minded people, differs from the quest of the masses. They like nothing better, and in their

silliness, enjoy nothing more, than to set the Law and reason at opposite ends, and to move everything far from explicable. So they claim it to be a miracle, and they shrink from identifying it as a natural incident, whether it is something that happened in the past and is recorded, or something predicted to happen in the future.

But I try to reconcile the Law and reason, and wherever possible consider all things as of the natural order. Only when something is explicitly identified as a miracle, and reinterpretation of it cannot be accommodated, only then I feel forced to grant that this is a miracle (*Resurrection*, p. 223).

Note that this is a weaker criterion for figurative interpretation of scripture than offered before in the case of the creation narrative. There the presumption was to accept the literal meaning of scripture unless it conflicted with demonstrated truth, or unless an alternative interpretation would destroy a foundation of the Law, or conflict with prophetic claims. Here, by contrast, Maimonides' inclination is to provide a natural explanation of a scriptural miracle report unless he is "forced" to grant that it is a miracle, although there are times when he is uncertain whether scripture reports a genuine miracle or not. In *Guide* 2.29 he explains figuratively many of the miracles that appear to involve a permanent change in nature at the end of days, or during the messianic period.

For Maimonides, the regularities of nature proclaim the glory of God more impressively than the exceptions. Miracles are beneficial either because they teach us a lesson (such as God's power to suspend nature), or provide evidence for a prophet, or motivate our action. The divine promises and threats of miraculous occurrences (e.g., that the Israelites will receive rain if they observe the Law) motivate people who otherwise may not scrupulously perform commandments, just as promising a child money or candy induces him to practice the piano. The actual fulfillment of the promises and threats also motivate people.[9]

Given Maimonides' devaluation of miracles, it is not surprising that some of the radical esotericists have questioned whether he genuinely accepted their possibility. Other scholars grant their possibility, but question whether he believed that any had actually occurred.[10] The best evidence they have is a passage in his *Commentary on the Mishnah*, where it is stated that ever since creation all things have proceeded according to their natures. A midrash is cited to the effect that miracles had been placed by God within the natures of things at creation so that they when they occurred later, it would *seem* to people that they had occurred in response to a need. If Maimonides agrees with the midrash (and this is not clear in the context of the passage), then this would constitute a naturalistic interpretation of miracles (2.29, pp. 345–6).

The difficulty is that Maimonides characterizes the same midrash in the *Guide* as "very strange," although he praises the rabbis for wishing to deny that any new nature comes to be, or that God's will changes. In other words, he praises them for their *intentions* in defending the stability of nature and the immutability of God, but not for the *actual* explanation of miracles.[11] I think that Maimonides was inclined to accept the rabbinic explanation of miracles at the time of the writing of the *Commentary on the Mishnah*, and that he later distanced himself from it because of his increasing emphasis on the creation of the world *ex nihilo* and *post nihilum*, and God's mastery over nature. His later writings do not differ significantly from the *Guide*; indeed, some of the same points are made more forcefully: In the *Medical Aphorisms* he says that the eternity-thesis excludes God having "novel volitions" (*Medical Aphorisms*, vol. 2, p. 216), which, he implies, are required for miracles as he understands them.

In any event, Maimonides' disinclination to accept the rabbinic explanation of miracles (i.e., their being embedded within things from creation) is inferred from another passage in *Guide* 2.29. After offering a figurative explanation of Isaiah's prophecy that God will create "new heavens and a new earth" after the restoration of the Jewish kingdom (Isaiah 65:17), he writes:

> Even he who takes "new heavens and a new earth" to mean what people think it means says: "Even the heavens and earth that will be created in the future are already created and subsist, for it is said: they subsist before me. It is not said: they will subsist, but: they subsist" (Joel 2:11). And he quotes in proof his saying: "There is nothing new under the sun." (Ecclesiastes 1:9). Do not think that this is in contradiction to what I have explained. For it is possible that he means that the nature that will necessitate in time the states of existence that have been promised, is created since the six days of the Beginning. And this is true.

> I have said that a thing does not change its nature in such a way that the change is permanent merely in order to be cautious with regard to the miracles....

Here Maimonides contrasts the emergence of already-created natures with the occurrence of miracles, i.e., the temporary suspension of existing natures. If anything is embedded in the world from the time of existing natures. If anything is embedded in the world from the time of creation, says Maimonides, it is natures and not miracles.

Divine Knowledge

Since the impersonalist theory of providence does not *require* a God that interferes in the workings of the world, it may seem surprising that Maimonides insists on God's knowing particular humans (3.20–21) or on His power to work miracles. A king who has created just legal institutions does not need to see every suspected criminal, nor alter those institutions, in order for justice to be dispensed.

Why, then, the insistence on the divine power to suspend nature, or on a divine knowledge that encompasses "the circumstances of humans"? In the case of miracles we have already heard Maimonides' answer: the Bible provides ample evidence for miraculous events, evidence that cannot be interpreted away unless one engages in "crazy imaginings."

The issue of God's knowledge appears to be similar for Maimonides. After arguing for a divine omniscience that includes particulars within its scope, Maimonides maintains that "those who adhere to a Law" accept five features of God's knowledge that differentiate it from human knowledge:

1. God's knowledge is unitary, yet it corresponds to many known things belonging to various species.
2. God's knowledge is actual, yet some of its objects are potential, i.e., do not yet exist.
3. God's knowledge may have as its object the infinite.
4. God's knowledge is immutable, yet some of its objects are changing.
5. God's knowledge may be of the future possible event, which nonetheless remains possible (3.20, pp. 482–83).

Maimonides does not explain how he arrives at these features, except to say that the fifth is clear to him from the texts of the Torah. In fact, he has transformed five philosophical paradoxes of God's knowledge of external things that he had himself listed (Cf. 3.16, p. 463) into the very features that we attribute to God!

Of course, one would expect Maimonides to justify attributing these features to God despite their paradoxical nature, instead of acting like the philosophers and using the paradoxes to deny them of God. He does that with a rather neat argument, one he had employed also in the *Commentary on Mishnah* and the *Mishneh Torah*. Briefly put, the argument goes as follows: the philosophers themselves had shown that we cannot comprehend God's existence completely. Now, God's knowledge is identical with His existence. So it stands to reason that we cannot comprehend God's knowledge completely. The philosophers of all people should have realized that the manner of God's knowledge is unfathomable, and hence that the paradoxical features of God's knowledge are due to our ignorance rather than to some intrinsic contradictions (3.20, pp. 481–84).

By "comprehend God's knowledge completely" Maimonides means something like "comprehend adequately *how* God knows what He knows" or perhaps, "comprehend adequately what it is about God's knowledge (i.e., its nature) that explains how He knows what it knows." Maimonides does not elaborate, but it may be that the sort of comprehension he has in mind is what Aristotle calls *epistemê*, the understanding of something through its necessitating/explanatory causes. We cannot understand God's existence (=His essence), because among other things such an understanding would require knowledge of the causes of God's existence, and, "His existence has no causes through which He can be known."[13]

This approach is maddening to philosophically-minded readers who would prefer to be presented with an ingenious solution to the philosophical puzzles of divine omniscience rather than with a philosophical shrug of the shoulders. If all Maimonides can answer to these puzzles is "These matters are deep and beyond our comprehension," then how does he differ, say, from the pious theologian who takes refuge in the "inscrutable ways of God" when he is at a loss for words?

Part of our answer is that Maimonides, unlike the pious theologian, gives a philosophical argument to justify his skeptical stance. He also resists the temptation to adopt weak and unconvincing solutions on theological matters. We saw that Maimonides prefers his own probabilistic proofs of the createdness of the world to the demonstrations of the Kalam theologians, and he generally feels that no argument is better than a bad one. Here, too, he mentions one or two philosophical solutions before he dismisses them with his general skeptical argument.

Another part of the answer is that Maimonides' "agnosticism" is, as we saw before, restricted to justifying the lack of a convincing philosophical explanation, rather than to forestall philosophical speculation. If one looks at the various topics in which he appeals to God's unknowable essence or His inscrutable will, e.g., the theory of attributes, the doctrine of creation, and his statements on God's knowledge of external things, the appeal to the agnostic argument always comes *after* we have reached a philosophical impasse.

72

Were Maimonides to be committed to a stronger agnosticism, then it would be hard to see how he could claim to know, for example, that God knows future contingents without altering their contingency. He bases that claim in *Guide* 3.20 on the texts of the Torah, and the import of the "whole of religious legislation, the commandments, and the prohibitions," and he suggests that beliefs in God's omniscience and the contingency of human action are rationally grounded, the latter doctrine being taught by philosophy and Torah.[14]

Or when he claims, for example, that our intellect cannot comprehend the divine intellect, he does not thereby mean that we cannot demonstrate that God is pure intellect in actuality, or that God is knower, knowledge, and object known. What he appears to mean is that we cannot understand what it is about the nature of the divine essence that makes God these things. Similarly, in the case of divine knowledge, we can show that God's knowledge is unitary, prior to experience, productive, etc. But we cannot understand what it is about the nature of the divine essence that makes God's knowledge this way.

Because Maimonides does not, like Kant, provide a priori arguments to demarcate sharply the boundaries of human knowledge, we have no choice but to examine his views on each issue in order to appreciate what he feels can and cannot be known. Thus when faced with the divine knowledge/contingency of human action puzzle (i.e., if God knows what I will do tomorrow, am I able to do otherwise?), he rejects all solutions, preferring instead to appeal to the agnostic argument in order to justify our inability to know how God knows the world. Yet he insists that God knows things external to Himself through knowing Himself, since the existence of those things depends on Him. This suggests that he was aware of the problem of God's knowing external things, and that he perhaps was influenced by the philosophical response given by some of his predecessors.[15]

The upshot of all this is that we cannot scientifically understand what it is about the nature of the divine essence that makes God's knowledge the way it is:

> For us to desire to have an intellectual cognition of the way this comes about [how God knows the totality of what derives from His acts through His knowing Himself] is as if we desired that we be He and our apprehension be His...It is impossible for us to know in any way this kind of apprehension. (3.21, p. 485)

That we cannot understand how God knows the world does not imply that we cannot know through demonstration many propositions about His knowledge of the world, including that He knows the world through knowing Himself. Knowledge yes, scientific understanding, no.

Summary

According to Maimonides, Biblical statements about divine providence, communication, reward and punishment, etc., are true when properly interpreted. That interpretation involves, for the most part, transferring what the Bible attributes to a personal God to impersonal, *natural* processes—for such processes are what the Bible truly intends when it refers to God's "actions." He explains these actions with the aid of elements of the medieval neo-Aristotelian worldview. Thus, God's governance of the sublunary world is explained in terms of the latter's constant cycle of generation and corruption; prophecy as the natural communication of truths via the active intellect to the human intellect and imagination; special providence, as consequent upon the intellectual bond between the human and the divine. Still, by offering a naturalistic explanation of the way God relates to the world, Maimonides does not wish to deny supernatural phenomena such as miracles and miraculous providence. Their importance lies in their showing God's mastery over nature. For God, although not a person, is an intelligent, volitional, and intentional agent.

The naturalist interpretation of divine action runs into difficulties when Maimonides encounters the question of undeserved suffering. Perhaps we can see why from an admittedly trivial example. Consider the parents who, in order to limit their child's television viewing on school nights, install a timer to shut off the television set at 8 PM. They tell their child to stop watching television at 8 and then do her homework. At first, the child thinks the shut-off to be a coincidence; then she thinks that her parents are somehow watching her and turning off the television set as a punishment for attempting to see more than her allotted time. Although she cannot figure out how they do it, she is willing to concede that the punishment is deserved.

But one day the child decides to do her homework first, so she can watch a program at 8 PM ; the timer again shuts the television off at 8. Why, she asks her babysitter who arrives at 8:30, did she deserve to suffer; after all, she had already done her homework? The babysitter may reply that the suffering was not deserved, that her parents are not omniscient or omnipotent, and that they do the best they can. Or that her parents are mean and unfair. Or that her suffering was somehow deserved because she should not have decided to do the homework early. Or that missing television was not a punishment at all, since too much television is injurious to her mental health and ultimate happiness.

Maimonides does not, cannot reply that God is not omnipotent or omniscient or just. As long as he holds that all events befalling humans are deserved, then he must take refuge in the inscrutable connection between divine ways and human actions. Later in the *Guide* he implies that evils befall humans because they cannot escape their corporeality. As long as humans do not strengthen the intellectual bond between them and God, they are subject to the "whips and scorns of outrageous fortune." Fortunately, Maimonides feels that by strengthening the bond, these whips and scorns lose their sting.

Endnotes

[1] Cf. Seeskin 2000, 143–146.

[2] Rahman 1958 is still useful for background.

[3] For details, see Walzer 1969.

[4] For a thorough analysis of all texts of Maimonides relevant to prophecy, see Kreisel 2001.

[5] See Pines's "Translator's Introduction" to the *Guide of the Perplexed*, pp. lxxxix-ciii.

[6] See Kaplan 1977.

[7] Hyamson's translation: "of himself," adding in a footnote, "without divine authority." Cf. *Introduction to Helek*, pp. 420–1.

[8] There is a lot of literature (and one recent Hebrew dissertation) on this topic.

[9] That God has meted out reward and punishment miraculously according to the "promises and threats" of the Law is strongly implied in 3.32, p. 528: "and performing in deed all these acts of benefiting and all these acts of vengenace."

[10] See Seeskin 2000, p. 183. It is not the case that Maimonides argues only for the *possibility* of miracles, and then turns skeptical once he has established that possibility.

[11] Kasher 1998, p. 38.

[12] What follows is based on Manekin 2002.

[13] Ibid. Cf. *Guide* 1:52, p. 115.

[14] *Commentary on the Mishnah: Introduction to Avot* 8, ed. Y. Kafih, p. 397.

[15] For example, Themistius. See Pines 1996, p. 288ff., who gives several examples of possible direct and indirect influence.

6
Human Happiness

For most of the Guide Maimonides has much to say about the *views* his readers should hold, but relatively little about the *lives* they should lead. At the end of the book, however, he addresses those readers who have perfected their intellectual and moral virtues, and who have understood and accepted his teachings until that point. He urges them to foster an attitude towards God and His works that that is aptly called "intellectual worship" (3.51, p. 623). To appreciate the end of the Guide we must first take a detour through Maimonides' other writings. Like so many other thinkers, Maimonides assumes that to understand how humans are to live their lives, we must first understand what sort of creatures they are.

Human Biology and Psychology

Maimonides accepts Aristotle's definition of humans as rational animals. As animals they are composed of bodies containing flesh, bones, various mixtures, bodily organs, and animal spirits, parts that are ruled and parts that are ruling, chief of which is the heart. The parts of the individual body are joined by a force that governs them and provides for their preservation and well-being, which is called nature, i.e., the nature of the individual living human body (1.72, pp. 187–88). The functions of the body are the parts or faculties of the soul, of which there are five: nutritive, sentient, imaginative, appetitive, and rational. They do not constitute different souls but are different powers of one soul, which is the functioning of the human body as a whole.

Although we speak of "body" and "soul," the two should not be viewed as distinct substances, and, indeed, when the body dies, most of its functioning ceases. What survives of the human soul after the body we shall examine below.

Maimonides, it will be recalled, was a practicing physician, and he wrote medical treatises that covered the gamut of physical, psychological, and emotional problems. His medical approach plays a decisive role in his ethics, because "the improvement of the moral habits (*ahlaq*) is the same as the cure of the soul and its powers" (*Eight Chapters* 1, p. 61). In order to preserve and maintain the health of the soul, one has to preserve and maintain the health of the body. Of course, as we just saw, the body has a built-in guiding force, its nature, that keeps it going. But due to its corporeality, the body is composed of contrary elements that ultimately lead to its decomposition and destruction. The task of each individual, under the guidance of a physician, is to adopt a regimen that will maintain, as much as possible, the balance of these elements, so that one does not gain ascendancy over the other.

This task is viewed by Maimonides as a religious imperative, derived from the Biblical injunction to walk in God's ways (Deut. 28:9). For among God's "ways" are understanding and knowledge, and "to attain understanding and knowledge is impossible when one is sick" (*Character Traits* 4:1, p. 36). So Maimonides presents a general health regimen in his *Code of Law*, the only Jewish codifier to do so. One finds prescribed therein, for example, daily exercise (until the body has warmed up, after which a cooling down period must follow), weekly baths (with a detailed procedure on how one should bathe), and certain healthy foods (and combinations of foods). Unhealthy foods (and combination of foods) are listed and forbidden. There are remedies for constipation ("a leading cause for illness according to the physicians") and warnings against excessive sexual activity (another leading cause); in general, a man should engage in sexual intercourse only when strong and healthy, and then only for therapeutic reasons (Ibid. 4:19, p. 40).

This last stricture on sexual activity should be noted. Although Maimonides recognizes the traditional imperatives of procreation and marital sex in rabbinic Judaism, his ultimate concern here is for the health and well-being of the body so that the mind is able to know and to understand. While he cites general principles of physical health in his *Code of Law*, he underscores that individuals should undertake his regimen under the guidance of a physician, who can adapt his therapies to individuals. In places where there are no physicians, his principles will be of benefit to both the well and the ill.

Maimonides precedes his discussion of physical health in his *Code of Law* with a discussion of psychological health, at the center of which is his analysis of human *"de'ot,"* his own Hebrew coinage for "character traits" or "ethical dispositions" (the root of *"de'ot* is *yd-'* "to know").[1] Examples given are irascibility, haughtiness, meekness, miserliness, etc. Some of these traits are closely connected to one's physical constitution and hence are virtually innate, others are acquired through an individual's predisposition, or through training and imitation. The purpose of Maimonides' analysis is to evaluate the traits with an eye to an individual's psychological well-being, and to offer the proper regimen by which harmful traits can be eradicated, and positive traits can be reinforced and fostered.

Rather than analyze each positive trait, Maimonides presents as a general principle that "the right way is the mean in every single one of a man's character traits. It is the character trait that is equally distant from the extremes" (*Character Traits* 1:4, p. 29). This is ambiguous; it could mean that each character trait has a mean, or that there are certain traits that are by their very nature "mean traits." Yet the ambiguity is more apparent than real. Maimonides believes that character traits can be measured in terms of excess, deficiency, and moderation; whether we characterize a man as "generous" or "moderately giving" is of little importance.

Of course, if we took literally Maimonides' notion that the right way is the mean in every one of man's character traits, then we could understand him as advising the lazy man to be moderately lazy or the temperate man to be only moderately so. But this is not his intent, as he goes on to say:

> [One] shall only desire the things which the body needs and without which it is impossible to live...likewise he shall only labor at his work to acquire what he needs for the present....He shall not be extremely tightfisted nor squander all his wealth, but he shall give charity according to his means....This way is the way of the wise men....Whoever is exceedingly scrupulous with himself and moves a little toward one side or the other, away from the character trait in the mean, is called a pious man. (Ibid, 1:4–5, p. 29)

The wise seek the mean; the virtuous or the pious[2] diverge from the mean towards an extreme, but as a prophylactic measure, i.e., in order to maintain their psychic well-being.[3] A diseased soul is one in which vices have taken grip; to eradicate them one needs to employ therapies that often involve extreme measures. The virtuous or the pious know themselves and their character traits, and so they will diverge in their actions from the mean in order to achieve the proper balance.

The view of the virtues as mean character traits was no doubt familiar to Maimonides from his reading of the *Nicomachean Ethics*, as well as from certain ethical treatises of Alfarabi, where it was also taught within the context of human psychology.[4] But unlike Aristotle, who devotes much space to the analysis of virtues and vices, Maimonides concentrates on the practical question of how to acquire the former and to rid oneself of the latter. Once again the emphasis is on the therapeutic; after laying down general guidelines he exhorts his reader to seek the guidance of a "physician of the soul," for just as the same medicine may cure or harm, so too the same psychological therapy. And just as one knowledgeable in medicine is constantly monitoring his body for signs of illness or weakness, so too the virtuous man should inspect his moral habits daily for signs of weakness or decay.

Observing the Law, which contains "just and equibalanced statutes," fosters the acquisition of the mean character traits that constitute the virtues. Maimonides appears to rely less than Aristotle on the ability of the virtuous man to know how to act, but that may be because he recognizes the existence of the Law of the perfect virtuous man, Moses, as the ultimate guide for life.

Psychophysical Equilibrium and the Extinction of Desire

Maimonides' view of the virtues as mean character traits has been the subject of intense and critical discussion. Some have suggested that the doctrine is intended as a "baseline morality" for the multitude but not for the elite.[5] They observe that the fullest discussions of the middle way occur in his legal writings,[6] that there are passages (especially in the *Guide*) that present a more positive approach to ascetic modes of behavior, that Maimonides' requirement of complete devotion to the knowledge and service of God goes beyond the doctrine of the mean. Other scholars talk of contradictions, or at the very least tensions, in the presentations of various virtues and vices, that reflect an ambivalence about the mean. For example, Maimonides says both that one should only become angry where it is appropriate to do so, and that one should always avoid anger. Finally, the doctrine of the mean has come in for its share of criticism as promoting "mediocrity" or "middlingness" in ethics[7] (another reason, perhaps, for arguing that Maimonides abandons it in the end).

All these problems stem from a misunderstanding of the doctrine of the mean and its place in Maimonides' philosophy. Maimonides does not view the possession of mean character traits as an end in itself; he certainly does not treat the maxim "Be moderate" as a universal principal of morality derived from reason. He is concerned rather with the psychophysical well-being of individuals that is necessary for them to achieve their goal in life, which he formulates as "the mental representation of the intelligibles [=the eternal truths and concepts], the most certain and noble of which being the apprehension, insofar as it is possible, of God, the angels, and His other works" (3.8, pp. 432–33). In order to achieve the end for which they are created, people need to first achieve psychophysical equilibrium, and this is the whole purpose of acquiring the mean character traits.

This emerges clearly from Maimonides' description of the stages of the development of that most perfect of humans, the prophet. First he is born as a human individual whose brain is "extremely well proportioned because of the purity of its matter and of the particular temperament of each of its part." Then he obtains knowledge and wisdom until he acquires "a perfect and accomplished human intellect and pure and well-tempered human moral habits." Only when this psychophysical equilibrium has been achieved will

> all his desires be directed to acquiring the science of the secrets of what exists and knowledge of its causes…By then, he will have detached his thought from, and abolished his desire for, bestial things—I mean the preference for the pleasures of eating, drinking, and sexual intercourse, and, in general, of the sense of touch….(2.36, p. 371)

Note that far from being opposed to the elimination of physical desire, psychophysical equilibrium is its necessary condition. Or to put this differently, without the possession of the mean character traits, the extinction of desire required of the perfected individual is impossible.

Natural vs. Conventional Morality

Like the Greeks before him Maimonides finds the principle of temperance and equibalance in nature, and he accepts the notion that man is a microcosm of the world (1.72, p. 190). So in this very important sense, the doctrine of the mean character traits forms the basis of a natural morality for Maimonides, one to be contrasted with a conventional morality that often varies from people to people and from culture to culture.[8] Moral judgments that are based on cultural norms carry weight when they improve the well-being of the individual or the society. For example, he writes that heavy drinking is more disgraceful than group defecation in public, "for excreting is a necessary thing that man cannot refrain from by any device whatever, whereas being drunk is an act committed by a bad man in virtue of his choice" (3.8, p. 434). Excessive drinking is harmful to the body and hence bad (natural morality), but the uncovering of the private parts is "most manifestly bad" (1.2, p. 25) because of a "generally accepted opinion" (conventional morality). The intellect determines the former and is neutral on the latter.

This devaluation of conventional morality underlies Maimonides' interpretation of Adam's fall in the second chapter of the Book of Genesis (1.2) In the Biblical story Adam and Eve eat from the forbidden tree of the knowledge of good and evil, whereupon they become aware and ashamed of their nakedness. This puzzled a certain "learned man" who asked Maimonides how Adam, as a consequence of his disobedience, could receive the greatest gift humans possess, the intellect, with its capacity to distinguish between good and evil. After all, the man reasoned, prior to their sin Adam and Eve had roamed about as oblivious to their nakedness as the beasts. Why reward their transgression?

Maimonides answer is that Adam's sinning did not result in his acquisition of intellect, but rather in his acquisition of the faculty of judging things to be fine and disgraceful, i.e., the basis for conventional morality. Adam had been created with an intellect whose objects are the intelligibles (eternal truths), but he preferred the senses whose objects are material objects of desire. He preferred knowledge of conventional morality over that of philosophy and science, and thus he was punished rather than rewarded.

Maimonides does not treat the story of the fall of Adam as history but rather an allegory for the human condition, although he is reticent to reveal the secrets of his interpretation (2.30, p. 355). Some of his commentators read him as saying that humans (Adam), because of their corporeality, constantly succumb to desire and imagination (the serpent), and hence inevitably fall from their state of uninterrupted intellectual apprehension (the Garden of Eden). Only by great endeavor ("by the sweat of your brow") are they able to apprehend the intelligibles ("you will bring forth bread," Gen. 3:19).[9]

The Well-Balanced Society

Although Maimonides holds that particular human societies are arranged by convention and not by nature, the social body functions in ways similar to the human body, and hence is in need of order and equilibrium, which its ruler and laws provide. Maimonides uses almost the same language to describe the tasks of the ruler as he does to describe the tasks of the physician of the soul:

> [The ruler] gauges the actions of individuals, perfecting that which is deficient and reducing that which is excessive, prescribing actions and moral habits that all of them must always practice in the same way, so that the natural diversity is hidden through the multiple points of conventional accord, and so the community becomes well ordered. (2.40, p. 382)

The ruler's goal is not to stamp out diversity, which is impossible given the vast differences between individuals, but to provide "multiple points of conventional accord" that will provide for the harmonious functioning of society. His goal is the well-balanced society.

But what is the goal of a well-balanced society? Since the modern period there have been political theorists who claim that no further goal is needed; according to them the task of the ruler (or the government) is to provide individuals with the maximum amount of liberty to further their own pursuits, while protecting the rights of other individuals and groups within the society to do the same.

Maimonides thinks otherwise. Societies are constituted by laws, and the law whose only goal is to create a well-ordered and just society is human and imperfect. The divine law shares this goal, but also seeks to instill in society's members correct beliefs, perfecting their rational faculty, and directing them to speculative matters. This is the kind of law "that takes pains to inculcate correct opinions with regard to God...and angels, and that desires to make man wise, to give him understanding, and to awaken his attention, so that he should know the whole of that which exists in its true form" (2.40, p. 348). Or as he writes elsewhere, "The divine law as a whole has two aims—the welfare of the body and the welfare of the soul," (3.27, p. 510), the former being a necessary condition for the latter.

To demonstrate this last claim Maimonides devotes around twenty-five chapters to analyzing the wisdom inherent in the Torah and its precepts (3.26–50). He is aware that searching for the "explanations of the commandments"—by which he means the benefit that accrues from the observance of the commandments—is not an uncontroversial topic. There are those who think that any attempt to fathom the divine imperatives somehow makes God Himself comprehensible. But he rejects this line of reasoning. God does nothing, or decrees nothing, without a goal or intended benefit, although sometimes that benefit is difficult to discover. Hence, *all* the commandments of the Torah have explanations, i.e., beneficial ends. Maimonides rejects viewing the rabbinic distinction between *mishpatim* (laws) and *huqqim* (statutes) as one between those commandments that have beneficial ends and those that do not. Rather, he suggests that the *mishpatim* possess ends whose utility is manifest to all, whereas the *huqqim* possess ends whose utility is manifest only to the wise, sometimes only after great study. Even the particulars (i.e., details) have beneficial ends, although Maimonides considers it an idle exercise to search for the reasons of some particulars, for example, why a ram is mandated for a particular sacrifice rather than a lamb, or why seven lambs rather than eight. Unfortunately, he does not tell us *which* sorts of particulars lack good explanations, nor can that be inferred from his examples. And he himself explains why certain sacrifices require young rather than old turtle doves, and why others require male rather than female sheep.[10]

All this should be reminiscent of Maimonides' discussion of divine will and creation, where he claimed that once we accept the idea that God particularizes the world according to what His wisdom requires, then questions like "Why are there nine celestial spheres rather than eight?" cease to trouble the scientist, or, as we interpreted it, the *lack* of a convincing answer ceases to trouble the scientist. For that question is apparently beyond the scope of convincing explanation. What determines the number of spheres is God's will—not an arbitrary will, but a will that is consequent upon divine wisdom. Similarly, in the case of commandments: Maimonides claims that

> Wisdom rendered it necessary—or, if you will, say that necessity occasioned—that there should be particulars for which no cause can be found; it was, as it were, impossible in regard to the Law that there should be nothing of this class in it. In such a case the impossibility is due to the circumstances that when you ask why a lamb should be prescribed and not a ram, the same question would have to be asked if a ram had been prescribed instead of a lamb. But one particular species had to be chosen....This resembles the nature of the possible, for it is certain that one of the possibilities will come to pass. And no question should be put why one particular possibility and not another comes to pass, for a similar question would become necessary if another possibility instead of this particular one had come to pass...(3.26, p. 509).

Some have interpreted Maimonides as saying that God's choice of the lamb rather than the ram is arbitrary. But it is more likely that he holds that while one can explain why a certain type of animal is chosen, no explanation can be provided why that type *must* be chosen rather than another type, either because of the limitation of human intellect, or because of Maimonides' Aristotelian conviction that certain things in law, as in nature, are irreducibly possible.

We should pause to consider one particularly controversial aspect of Maimonides' treatment of the *huqqim*, which he expands beyond the rabbinic understanding of the term to include all the sacrificial rites, the Temple cult, laws of ritual purity and impurity, as well as agricultural laws, and some other commandments. Maimonides maintains that the *huqqim* were promulgated by Moses because the Israelites had been steeped in the idolatrous views and practices of the Sabians, a pagan nation whose culture, Maimonides believed, dominated the ancient world during Biblical times. This explains why only the wise are able to understand the benefits of many of the *huqqim*—only they possess the requisite knowledge of Sabian culture and practices to understand the historical framework of the commandments. But Maimonides' explanation raises several questions: Doesn't it confine the *huqqim* to a particular socio-historical context, thereby reducing their universality and significance as eternal commandments? What is the benefit in observing the sacrificial laws, for example, or wishing to restore their observance, after that context is no longer valid? And even if Maimonides considers the threat of "Sabianism" to be an ever-present one, why should the whole point of the Temple worship and the sacrifices be merely to root our idolatrous practices and views? What about the Biblical notion that some sacrifices aim to propitiate God and of others to expiate sins?

By now this last question should not be difficult for us. We are accustomed to Maimonides' non-literal interpretation of scripture, his rejection of a personal God, his belief in divine immutability. The idea that humans can effect a change in the divine will through offering a burnt sacrifice is not qualitatively different from some of the Sabian superstitions that the Law was intended to root out. What is different is the object of worship. For Maimonides, idolatry—the acceptance or worship of something besides God as the deity—is the root of *all* untruth, superstition, and immorality. So it is no insignificant matter to say that the purpose of the sacrifices is to root out idolatrous practices and views; indeed, that is the purpose of all the *huqqim*, and not only them; "the first intention of the Law as a whole is to put an end to idolatry to wipe out its traces and all that is bound up with it, even its memory as well as all that leads to any of its works" (3.17, p. 519).

Why, then, does the Mosaic Law contain legislation that presupposes beliefs that are not only false, but tantamount to idolatrous, such as the notions that God delights in sacrifices, or that He can be appeased, etc., through burnt offerings? To answer this Maimonides advances a theory that he knows will arouse "a feeling of repugnance at first": he claims that the sacrificial laws were promulgated not for their own sake, but in order to wean the Israelites away from idol worship, since they had become accustomed to sacrifice as the preeminent mode of worship. The Torah mandated sacrifice as a concession to people's nature at the time. Still, by regulating the time, place, and manner of sacrifices, eliminating the abominations associated with it (such as child sacrifice), and redirecting it to the true deity, the "first intention of the Law" is satisfied.

Once again, Maimonides' answer should not surprise us. The false theological beliefs associated with sacrifice are not different in kind from those associated with petitional prayer—both assume, incorrectly, the existence of a God that literally responds to petitions and gifts. But just as the Mosaic Law does not forbid prayer, but on the contrary mandates it, finding it necessary, under certain circumstances, in order to point the way to a more meditative worship, so too it does not forbid sacrifice, but finds it necessary, under certain circumstances, in order to point the way to a more spiritual form of worship.

But what happens when those circumstances change? Committed as he is to the eternality of the Law—as much an expression of the unchanging divine will as is nature—Maimonides is committed to the eternal binding character of the *huqqim*. This does not mean that the application of the Law may not vary according to circumstances. The existence of the oral Law and the rabbinic tradition play a part in that application, as does the course of human history; after the destruction of the Second Temple in 70 AD the rabbis put the sacrificial system on hold until the rebuilding of the Temple. Maimonides famously rules in his *Code of Law* that the King Messiah will rebuild the Temple in Jerusalem and will reinstitute all the ancient laws, including sacrifices (*Kings and Wars*, 11:1). He does not mention whether the sacrifices will have the same purpose then as they originally did. Perhaps the restoration of the Temple and the sacrificial rite will have something to do with the preparation "of the entire world to serve the Lord with one accord." Whatever the benefit that Maimonides will find in the restoration of the Temple and the sacrificial and purity laws, "the one occupation of the whole world during the messianic age will be to know the Lord (*Kings and Wars*, 12:5). The knowledge of God, rather than the performance of the sacrificial rites at the Temple, will take center stage.

Maimonides has a very definite vision of the final end of humans. His ideal society allows for a certain amount of diversity—people necessarily differ from each other—but it is not a liberal nor a particularly tolerant one. If the Torah aims to inculcate certain beliefs, it also aims to eradicate other conflicting beliefs, and, if necessary, the proponents of those beliefs as well.[11]

Maimonides' *religious dogmatism*—we already noted that he was the first thinker to draw up a list of "principles of the Torah,"[12] including theological beliefs, that are incumbent upon every Jew to understand and accept—is out of sync with today's values of pluralism and tolerance. But it is inaccurate to view his dark pronouncements against theological heretics solely as instances of medieval religious intolerance. Instead, they stem from his rationalist philosophical principles. For, as we shall see, Maimonides views human happiness (including the immortality of the intellectual soul) as consequent upon the possession of eternally true beliefs. He also implies that some of these true beliefs can be apprehended by virtually anybody, although there are varying levels of apprehension, and certain knowledge of them is obtained only through rational proof. Hence he considers it an obligation not only for the elite to obtain these beliefs, but for the multitude as well. Yet because they cannot be known by non-philosophers with certainty, the multitude are the most susceptible to heretics and sectarians. So they must be taught as much as they can understand about the principles, and warned about their importance. Maimonides' philosophical rationalism, coupled with his faith in the multitude's ability to acquire a rudimentary knowledge of certain beliefs, led him to adopt a dogmatic stance.

Summing up to this point: our goal according to Maimonides is the apprehension of the intelligibles, and this apprehension includes the knowledge, in so far as it is possible, of God, the angels, and His other works. To achieve that end, we must have first achieved physical and psychological health, characterized in terms of well-being and equilibrium. And to achieve that end, it is best that we live in a well-ordered society, which provides for our needs and regulates intercourse between us.

Observance of the "just and equibalanced" commandments of the Torah ensure that individual humans achieve, to the best of their abilities, the subsidiary ends of physical, psychological, and social well-being (3.27). But what makes the law uniquely divine is that it also teaches the correct doctrines necessary for the apprehension of the intelligibles. Since these doctrines appear in the Law in the form of allegories and parables, they need to be explained according to the intellectual capacity of the audience. Those fortunate enough to deepen their understanding of these doctrines are encouraged to do so through the philosophical study, which alone provides certain and unshakable knowledge.

"The Thing that Remains"

Of all the faculties of the human soul, Maimonides instructs us, only the intellect is immortal. For the ultimate human perfection is the active contemplation of eternal truths, and "this is the only cause of permanent preservation" (3.27, p. 511). The other faculties are linked in some manner to the body, and so when the body dies, there is nothing that can preserve them.

These views are part of a centuries-old tradition in psychology and biology that traces its origin to Aristotle. Since Aristotle viewed soul as "the actuality of a natural body having life potentially within it" (*De Anima* 2:1 412a27) it followed for him that when a body ceased to exist, so did its soul. But he also suggested, in a notoriously cryptic passage in *De Anima* 3.5, that one faculty or function of the human soul, namely, intellect, when it is actively thinking, is both "present in the soul" and separate (or separable) from the body, immortal, and eternal. So it became the task of his commentators to explain the nature of intellect, especially the nature of the "actively thinking intellect" and its relationship to the passive intellect, and to see whether this theory provided the basis for the belief in the immortality of the soul.

The Muslim Aristotelians, following some of their Greek predecessors, viewed the active intellect as an eternal incorporeal intelligence that plays a causal role in human cognition, and in the generation of sublunary entities. Although this interpretation of the active intellect seemed to condemn the human intellect to oblivion upon death (since the active intellect alone was described as eternal) it actually provided a way for its survival. For the question became how the human intellect can somehow participate in the active intellect's eternality. One suggestion was that the human intellect, once it has acquired all or most of the eternal truths and concepts, actually *conjoins* with the active intellect. In at least some of his writings Averroes answers that the human intellect can have the active intellect as the object of its thought, thereby conjoining in some manner with it, and shedding the human intellect's personality.[13]

Maimonides did not follow this path; at least he does not require any conjunction with the active intellect over and beyond what the mind receives of the intelligibles during ordinary cognition of the eternal truths. It seems that for him, once the intellect has moved from potentiality to actuality, i.e., once a number of eternal truths have been acquired, then the acquired intellect constitutes what he calls "the thing that remains" (1.40, p. 90; 1.41, p. 91; 3.22, p. 488).

The questions we have to ask about his doctrine are: a) What sort of thing is this "thing"? b) Does it have a distinct identity after the death of the body? and c) In what sense can we view it as the survival of something that existed *before* the death of the body?

Impersonal Immortality

Maimonides himself does not discuss questions a) and c), but he does have something to say about b): the intellects that survive are all *one* thing because there is nothing that can distinguish them from each other. Material individuals of the same species are distinguished by their material properties; separate intelligences are distinguished by one being the cause of another. But in the case of immortal intellects, which are non-material and not caused by each other, what could distinguish them (1.70, p. 174)? The difficulty with the argument, however, is that separate intelligences are distinguished *only* by the fact that one is the cause of another, whereas John's mind (i.e., his collection of eternal truths) is not the same as Mary's, even though some of the truths may be identical. This has led one scholar to suggest that Maimonides allows for varying levels of quality in the things that survive.[14] According to this interpretation, Maimonides' point is that the intellects that survive are all one *kind* of thing, or that they have a group identity while preserving some measure of specific distinctiveness.

Intellectual Survival and Continuity

What about the third question: in what sense is the "thing that remains" the survival of *my* soul? Imagine that you are told the good news that your soul is immortal, but that upon death you lose all your memories, perceptions, etc.; what survives is nothing but the theoretical knowledge you acquired during your life. Even assuming that you are satisfied with your knowledge of the Pythagorean theorem, in what sense is that knowledge *you*? Hasdai Crescas argued that if the acquired intellect existed, then it would have to be an entirely different substance, unconnected with the intellect prior to it. The prospect that upon death my intellect will be replaced by something entirely different and permanent may give me joy and comfort, but I can hardly see it as *my* survival.

Again, Maimonides does not address this issue, but a century and a half later, Gersonides did. He argued that the acquired intellect is constituted incrementally while the embodied soul is alive. With the removal of material impediments upon death, the acquired intellect is not substantially altered but rather united, or to use a computer metaphor, "defragmented." What guarantees that the "thing that remains" is identical with its mental ancestor is the mental continuity they share, which stretches back into the embodied life of the mind. This may be what Maimonides had in mind when he writes that the ultimate human perfection is

> the acquisition of the rational virtues—I mean, the conception of intelligibles...this is what gives the individual true perfection, a perfection belonging to him alone; *and it gives him permanent perdurance....*Therefore you ought to desire to achieve this thing, *which will remain permanently with you* (3.54, p. 637; emphasis added).

But this still does not seem satisfactory. For even assuming that the knowledge of the Pythagorean theorem that survives the death of my body is mentally continuous with the knowledge of the Pythagorean theorem which I acquired when I was fourteen, in what sense is that knowledge constitutive of my identity? How can I identify "the thing that remains" as the survival of *my self*?

It seems odd to us today how little these questions bothered medieval Jewish Aristotelians like Maimonides and Gersonides. But two observations may mitigate somewhat the oddity. First, Maimonides, like other premodern philosophers, does not work with the notion of a self that is the locus of our various activities. Thus, although he talks of the "acquired" intellect, there is no self that does the acquiring, no underlying "I" that is the subject of my thoughts. (This is not to say that Maimonides dispenses with the notion of an underlying subject, only that he does not identify that subject with what moderns call "the self.") Second, he does not view the intelligibles in the acquired intellect merely as subjectless objects (thoughts) or activities (thinkings). His acceptance of Aristotle's doctrine of the identity of subject, object, and act of intellect ensures that where there are intelligibles there is something that thinks them, and in fact, that the thinker and the thought are identical. So, the acquired intellect is substantive in the sense that the separate intellects are substantive; they are all *things thinking thoughts*, their "thingness" consisting entirely in their being active thinkers.

If this is correct, then we can answer questions a) and c): The "thing that remains" is a substance that emerges from the acquisition of the eternal truths, i.e., the acquired intellect. Since those truths are acquired during the embodied lifetime of the human intellect, there is mental continuity between the "thing that remains" and the intellect before the death of the body. Moreover, there is reason to believe that for Maimonides we experience this blessed state during our lifetime, although only for brief moments.

The "Intellectual Worship of God"

Let us assume that you have done everything that Maimonides has advised you to do. You have lived your life according to the ordinances of the Law; you have acquired the mean character traits; you have gained knowledge of the intelligibles. *Now* what do you do? This is the question that Maimonides poses at the end of the *Guide*, and at first glance it seems puzzling. What goal can be greater than the acquisition of eternal truths? Maimonides' answer appears simple: "Your continual contemplation of them." It is this continual contemplation that he calls "the intellectual worship of God," which requires "strengthening the bond between you and Him, which is the intellect" (3.51, p. 623)

This is not an easy task, considering the demands made upon us by our bodies, our families, and our communities. We saw above that Maimonides was wont to complain that his duties as physician and rabbi left him little time for philosophical investigation. Perhaps this is why he offers his readers strategies in the *Guide* to maximize the time they spend in the philosophical contemplation of God and His works. He exhorts them to prolong the time spent in the performance of certain commandments, such as prayer and the confession of God's uniqueness, in order to learn how to concentrate, which is necessary for contemplation. He speaks with admiration (and perhaps not a little envy) of Moses and the patriarchs who lived a life of social leadership "with their limbs only," but who inwardly were "always in His presence." In fact, their actions themselves constituted a worship of God, because they were devoted to the creation of a religious community that would worship, i.e., know God. Maimonides says that he cannot aspire to their rank, but he can aspire to the rank where one is able to concentrate intently on the intellectual worship of God. This is what he recommends to his readers.

Scholars have been puzzled by Maimonides' vision of the intellectual worship of God. On the one hand, some of his comments seem to imply that human happiness consists in engaging in solitary contemplation of the deity, and that this involves the withdrawal from society and its commitments, at least as an aspiration. On the other hand, Maimonides' models are Biblical leaders who themselves were occupied, at least "outwardly," with their families, tribes, and communities.

And although he claims that they attained a rank to which he cannot aspire, he himself lived a life of active social engagement.

Moreover, he maintains at the end of the *Guide* that the final goal of human life is not merely the apprehension of God, but also the apprehension of His works, i.e., the manner in which the world is brought into being and governed, with a view to assimilation to them. God's purpose is that "this should be our way of life" (3.54, p. 637). Does this constitute an eleventh-hour shift towards practical action within this world, an "ethical turn" that moves the philosopher away from the *via contemplativa*? Are perfected intellects required to return to the world, like the philosophers in Plato's parable of the cave, in order to fulfill their social responsibility to less fortunate humans? But what of their responsibility to their own continual contemplation of God?

A key to resolving these tensions—as much as they can be resolved—may be found in a careful reading of the distinction between apprehending God and apprehending His works (3.54, 637). By "apprehending God" Maimonides likely means apprehending truths that can be demonstrated concerning God, e.g., that He exists and is unique, incorporeal, unlike anything else. Perhaps he includes with "apprehending God" apprehending the perfections that philosophers predicate of God, e.g., "Intellect," "Necessary of Existence," "First Cause." Of course, he cannot mean apprehending God's essence, since "man shall not see Me and live" (1.64, p. 156). By "apprehending His works" Maimonides likely means apprehending His actions, which are the causes that serve as the instruments of God's bestowing existence on the world and its governance. Scripture refers to these attributes in the language of character traits (i.e., God is merciful, just, etc.), but, as we saw in chapter 2, this is a human projection. So the first thing we should note is that the imitation of God mentioned in the last pages of the *Guide* does not refer to the *acquisition* of character traits of graciousness, righteousness, and justice. For that would be relevant to moral perfection, which precedes and is inferior to intellectual perfection (3.54, p. 635).

Second, Maimonides explains that God is described in scripture as "gracious" because of the bestowal of existence, "righteous" because of the governance of the celestial and sublunary spheres, and "judge," because of "the occurrence in the world of relative good things and of relative great calamites, necessitated by judgment that is consequent upon wisdom" (3.54, p. 633). To apprehend these ways of God, then, is above all to know that the world is the product of a providential deity, or as Maimonides puts it, to know "His providence extending over his creatures as manifested in the act of bringing them into being and in their governance as it is."

Now Maimonides has said nothing so far about what humans should *do*, only about what some of them *know* when they have apprehended God's works. What happens to the knower *after* such knowledge has been acquired? On the "turn to the ethical" reading, the knower first apprehends the ethical attributes of God, and then resolves to act ethically in the world. He moves from theoretical knowledge to practical knowledge and finally arrives at action. But this is precisely how Maimonides understood the story of Adam's sin and fall! He cannot mean that the bond between God and humans—which is only via the *theoretical* intellect—is to be broken, only to be replaced by a life of practical actions. There can be no turn to the ethical at the end of the *Guide*, not in the way Maimonides understands that term.

But knowledge of God's works does have consequences for the perfected individual's conduct:

> The way of life of such an individual, after he has achieved this apprehension, will always have in view *loving-kindness, righteousness,* and *judgment,* through assimilation to His actions, may He be exalted, just as we have explained several times in this Treatise (3.54, p. 638).

Note that Maimonides does not claim that the perfected individual *ought* to have in view the three attributes of action, but that he *will,* i.e., as a consequence of his knowledge of God's works. There is no question of an ethical imperative here, or even a specific command to imitate God. *The imitation of God does not need to be commanded because it is a consequence of the apprehension of His works.* This may be understood as follows: in understanding how the world is governed and how existence flows from God, one is the recipient of the overflow of knowledge from the active intellect. If this overflow is received in abundance, then it continues from the perfected individual to others, as in the case of prophets who are "compelled" by virtue of their prophecy to teach their message to others (2:37, p. 375), a case that has aptly been called, "'overflowing' perfection."[15] The circumstances, including the preparedness, of the recipient of the overflow determine what shape it will take. But in any event the contemplation of God's works does not result in a static contemplation of a body of truths, but an *active* one that transforms a person's conduct and the course of her life. This activity mirrors the divine activity, and, as such, is grounded in contemplation of the eternal truths.

Endnotes

[1] See Septimus 2001, pp. 97–100, for discussion. Some of the character traits listed by Maimonides include emotions (e.g., anger), but emotions are not in themselves *de'ot* ; dogs can become angry, but I doubt that Maimonides' would consider canine anger to be a *de'ah*. Perhaps his choice of *de 'ah* implies the presence of a cognitive element through which the question of praise and blame becomes appropriate.

[2] Hebrew: *he-hasid*; in a parallel passage in the *Eight Chapters*, which was written in Judaeo-Arabic, the term is *al-fadil*, often translated as "the virtuous."

[3] The view of the deviation from the mean as a prophylactic measure is emphasized in the *Eight Chapters*, but I think it also implied in *Character Traits*. In any event, I do not wish to suggest that Maimonides subordinates the pious-type to the virtuous-type; they remain, as Daniel H. Frank points out, separate models.

[4] See Davidson 1977.

[5] See, e.g., Kreisel 1999, pp. 178–180.

[6] See Davidson 1963.

[7] See Schwarzschild 1990.

[8] Maimonides does not use the phrases "natural morality" or "conventional morality."

[9] Cf. Efodi's commentary *ad loc.*

[10] For this point, and indeed, for a masterly analysis of Maimonides' treatment of the explanations of the commandments, see Stern 1998, which has influenced the next two paragraphs. Stern, however, links his discussion with the esoteric/exoteric distinction.

[11] See Kellner 1999, pp. 52–65.

[12] See also Hyman 1967.

[13] See Davidson 1992, pp. 335–338.

[14] See Altmann 1987, p. 90.

[15] See Kreisel 1999, p. 135.

Bibliography

Works by Maimonides

The Code of Maimonides (*Mishneh Torah*): *The Book of Knowledge*:
Foundations of the Torah, Chs. 1–2. Trans. Bernard Septimus. In
The Jewish Philosophy Reader. Eds. Daniel H. Frank, Oliver
Leaman, and Charles H. Manekin. London and New York:
Routledge, 2000. *Character Traits*. Trans. Raymond Weiss. In
Ethical Writings of Maimonides. Eds. Raymond L. Weiss with
Charles Butterworth. New York: Dover, 1975. *Repentance*. In
Mishneh Torah: The Book of Knowledge by Maimonides. Ed. and
trans. Moses Hyamson. Jerusalem: Boys Town Jerusalem Publish-
ers, 1962. *Kings and Wars*. Trans. Abraham M. Hershman. In *A
Maimonides Reader*. Ed. Isadore Twersky. New York: Behrman
House, 1972.

*The Commentary on the Mishnah. Introduction to Helek: Sanhedrin,
Chapter Ten*. Trans. Arnold J. Wolf. In *A Maimonides Reader*. Ed.
Isadore Twersky. New York: Behrman House, 1972. *Eight Chap-
ters*. Trans. Charles Butterworth and Raymond Weiss. In *Ethical
Writings of Maimonides*. Eds. Raymond L. Weiss with Charles
Butterworth. New York: Dover, 1975.

The Essay on Resurrection. In *Crisis and Leadership: Epistles of Maimonides*. Trans. Abraham Halkin and discus. David Hartman. Phila-
delphia/New York/Jerusalem: Jewish Publication Society of
America, 1985).

The Guide of the Perplexed. Trans. Shlomo Pines. Chicago: University of
Chicago Press, 1963.

The Medical Aphorisms. Trans. Fred Rosner and Suessman Muntner. 2
vols. New York: Yeshiva University Press, 1971 and 1972.

Other Works

Abravanel, Isaac. *Principles of Faith*. Trans. Menachem Kellner. Oxford:
Littman Library of Jewish Civilization, 1982.

Altmann, Alexander. "Maimonides on the Intellect and the Scope of Metaphysics." In *Von der mittelalterlichen zur modernen Aufklärung.* Tübingen: J.C.B. Mohr (Paul Siebeck), 1987.

Baneth, D. "An Exchange of Letters of Maimonides." In *Studies in Memory of Asher Gulak and Samuel Klein.* Jerusalem: Hebrew University, 1942, pp. 50–56. (Heb.)

Benor, Ehud. "Meaning and Reference in Maimonides' Negative Theology." *Harvard Theological Review* 88 (1995): 339–60.

Broadie, Alexander. "Maimonides and Aquinas on the Names of God." *Religious Studies* 23 (1987): 157–70.

Burrell, David. *Knowing the Unknowable God: Ibn Sina, Maimonides, and Aquinas.* Notre Dame, Ind. University of Notre Dame Press, 1986.

Davidson, Herbert. *Alfarabi, Avicenna, and Averroes on intellect: their cosmologies, theories of the active intellect, and theories of human intellect.* Oxford: Oxford University Press, 1992.

——. "The Authenticity of Works Attributed to Maimonides." In *Me'ah She'arim: Studies in Medieval Jewish Spiritual Life in Memory of Isadore Twersky.* Eds. Ezra Fleischer, Gerald Blidstein, Carmi Horowitz, and Bernard Septimus. Jerusalem: Magnes, 2001, pp. 111–134.

——. "Maimonides' *Shemonah Peraqim* and al-Farabi's *Fusul al-Madani.*" *Proceedings of the American Academy for Jewish Research* 31 (1963): 33–50.

——. "The Middle Way in Maimonides' Ethics." *Proceedings of the American Academy of Jewish Research* 54 (1987): 31–72.

——. *Proofs for Eternity, Creation, and the Existence of God in Medieval Islamic and Jewish Philosophy.* New York: Oxford University Press, 1987.

Diamond, James Arthur. *Maimonides and the Hermenuetics of Concealment: Deciphering Scriptures and Midrash in the "Guide of the Perplexed."* Albany: SUNY Press, 2002.

Freudenthal, Gad. "Maimonides' Guide of the Perplexed and the Transmission of the Mathematical Tract 'On Two Asymptotic Lines" in the Arabic, Latin, and Hebrew Traditions.' In *Maimonides and the Sciences.* Eds. Hillel Levine and Robert S. Cohen. Dordrecht/Boston/London: Kluwer Publishers, pp. 35–56.

Gersonides (Levi ben Gershom). *The Wars of the Lord: Book Three: Divine Knowledge.* Trans. Seymour Feldman. Philadelphia/New York/Jerusalem: Jewish Publication Society, 1987.

Guttmann, Julius. *The Philosophy of Judaism.* Trans. David W. Silverman. Northvale, N.J.: Jason Aronson, 1988.

Hartman, David. *Maimonides: Torah and Philosophic Quest.* Philadelphia: Jewish Publication Society, 1976.

Hyman, Arthur. "Maimonides' 'Thirteen Principles.'" In *Jewish Medieval and Renaissance Studies*. Ed. A. Altmann. Cambridge, Mass.: Harvard University Press, 1967, pp. 119–44.

Ivry, Alfred. "Maimonides on Possibility." In *Mystics, Philosophers, and Politicians: Essays in Jewish Intellectual History in Honor of Alexander Altmann*. Eds. J. Reinharz and D. Swetschinski. North Carolina: Duke University Press, 1982.

Kaplan, Lawrence. "Maimonides on the Miraculous Element in Prophecy." *Harvard Theological Review* 70 (1977): 233–56.

Kasher, Hannah. "Biblical Miracles and the Universality of Natural Laws: Maimonides' Three Methods of Harmonization." *The Journal of Jewish Thought and Philosophy* 8 (1998): 25–52.

Kellner, Menachem. *Dogma in Medieval Jewish Thought*. New York: Oxford University Press, 1986.

——. *Must a Jew Believe Anything?* London: Littman Library of Jewish Civilization, 1999.

Klein-Braslavy, Sarah. "The Creation of the World and Maimonides' Interpretation of Gen. i–v." In Pines and Yovel, 1986.

——. *Maimonides' Interpretation of the Adam Stories in Genesis*. Jerusalem: Reuben Mass, 1986. (Heb.)

——. *Maimonides' Interpretation of the Story of Creation*. Jerusalem: Reuben Mass, 1987. (Heb.)

Kraemer, Joel. "Alfarabi's *Opinions of the Virtuous City* and Maimonides' *Foundations of the Law*." In *Studia Orientalia Memoriae D.H. Baneth Dedicata*. Eds. J. Blau, S. Pines, M. J. Kister, S. Shaked. Jerusalem: Magnes Press, 1979.

——. *Perspectives on Maimonides*. Oxford: Littman Library of Jewish Civilization, 1991.

——. "The Life of Moses ben Maimon." In *Judaism in Practice*. Ed. Lawrence Fine. Princeton, N.J.: Princeton U Press, 2001.

Kreisel, Howard. *Maimonides' Political Thought: Studies in Ethics, Law, and the Human Ideal.* Albany: SUNY Press, 1999.

——. *Prophecy: The History of an Idea in Medieval Jewish Philosophy*. Dordrecht/Boston/London: Kluwer Academic Publishers, 2001, pp. 148–311.

Langermann, Tzvi. "The True Perplexity: The *Guide of the Perplexed*: Part II, Chapter 24." In Kraemer 1991, pp. 159–174.

Lobel, Diana. "'Silence is Praise to You': Maimonides on Negative Theology, Looseness of Expression, and Religious Experience." *American Catholic Philosophical Quarterly* 76 (2002): 25–49.

Manekin, Charles H. "Belief, Certainty, and Divine Attributes in the *Guide of the Perplexed*." *Maimonidean Studies* 1 (1990): 117–142.

——. "Maimonides' on God's Knowledge—Moses of Narbonne's Averroist Reading." *American Catholic Philosophical Quarterly* 76 (2002): 52–74.

Pines, Shlomo. "The Philosophical Purport of Maimonides' Halachic Works and the Purport of the *Guide of the Perplexed*." In Pines and Yovel, 1986, pp. 1–14.

Pines, Shlomo and Yirmiyahu Yovel, eds. *Maimonides and Philosophy*. Dordrecht/Boston/Lancaster: Martinus Nijhoff, 1986.

Ravitzky, Aviezer. "The Secrets of the *Guide to the Perplexed*: Between the Thirteenth and Twentieth Centuries." In *Studies in Maimonides*. Ed. Isadore Twersky. Cambridge: Harvard University Press, 1990, pp. 159–207.

Saadia Gaon. *The Book of Beliefs and Opinions*. Trans. Samuel Rosenblatt. New Haven: Yale University Press, 1948.

Schwarzchild, Steven S. "Moral Radicalism and 'Middlingness' in the Ethics of Maimonides." Reprinted in *The Pursuit of the Ideal: The Jewish Writings of Steven Schwarzschild*. Ed. Menachem Kellner. Albany, NY: SUNY Press, 1990.

Shailat, I. *Maimonides' Introductions to the Mishnah*. 2nd Edition. Jerusalem, 1994. (Heb.)

——. *The Letters and Essays of Moses Maimonides*. 3rd Edition. 2 vols. Jerusalem, 1995. (Heb.)

Stern, Josef. "Logical Syntax as a Key to a Secret of the *Guide of the Perplexed*. *Iyyun* 38 (1989): 137–66.

——. *Problems and Parables of Law: Maimonides and Nachmanides on the Reasons for the Commandments*. Albany, NY: SUNY Press, 1998.

Strauss, Leo. *Persecution and the Art of Writing*. Glencoe, Il.: Free Press, 1952.

Stroumsa, Sarah. *The Beginnings of the Maimonidean Controversy in the East: Yosef Ibn Shim'on's Silencing Epistle Concerning the Resurrection of the Dead*. Jerusalem: Ben-Zvi Institute, 1999. (Heb.)

Twersky, Isadore, ed. *A Maimonides Reader*. New York: Behrman House, 1972.

——. *Introduction to the Code of Maimonides* (*Mishneh Torah*). New Haven/London. Yale University Press, 1980.

Walzer, Richard. "Al-Farabi's Theory of Prophecy and Divination." In *Greek into Arabic*. Cambridge, MA: Harvard University Press, 1969: 206–219.

Wolfson, Harry Austryn. "Maimonides and Gersonides on Divine Attributes as Ambiguous Terms." Reprinted in *Studies in the History of Philosophy and Religion*. 2 vols. Cambridge, Mass.: Harvard University Press, 1977, pp. 231–46.